Influenza Pandemics

Other titles in the World History Series

Influenza Pandemics

Lizabeth Hardman

LUCENT BOOKS
A part of Gale, Cengage Learning

GALE
CENGAGE Learning™

Detroit • New York • San Francisco • New Haven, Conn • Waterville, Maine • London

J614.518
Hardman

LIBRARY OF CONGRESS CATALOGING-IN-PUBLICATION DATA

Hardman, Lizabeth.
  Influenza pandemics / by Lizabeth Hardman.
     p. cm. -- (World history)
  Includes bibliographical references and index.
  ISBN 978-1-4205-0349-4 (hardcover)
  1. Influenza--History--Popular works. I. Title.
  RA644.I6H367 2011
  614.5'18--dc22

                                             2010035978

Lucent Books
27500 Drake Rd.
Farmington Hills, MI 48331

ISBN-13: 978-1-4205-0349-4
ISBN-10: 1-4205-0349-9

Printed in the United States of America
1 2 3 4 5 6 7 14 13 12 11 10

Printed by Bang Printing, Brainerd, MN, 1ˢᵗ Ptg., 01/2011

Contents

Foreword

Each year, on the first day of school, nearly every history teacher faces the task of explaining why his or her students should study history. Many reasons have been given. One is that lessons exist in the past from which contemporary society can benefit and learn. Another is that exploration of the past allows us to see the origins of our customs, ideas, and institutions. Concepts such as democracy, ethnic conflict, or even things as trivial as fashion or mores, have historical roots.

Reasons such as these impress few students, however. If anything, these explanations seem remote and dull to young minds. Yet history is anything but dull. And therein lies what is perhaps the most compelling reason for studying history: History is filled with great stories. The classic themes of literature and drama— love and sacrifice, hatred and revenge, injustice and betrayal, adversity and triumph—fill the pages of history books, feeding the imagination as well as any of the great works of fiction do.

The story of the Children's Crusade, for example, is one of the most tragic in history. In 1212 Crusader fever hit Europe. A call went out from the pope that all good Christians should journey to Jerusalem to drive out the hated Muslims and return the city to Christian control. Heeding the call, thousands of children made the journey. Parents bravely allowed many children to go, and entire communities were inspired by the faith of these small Crusaders. Unfortunately, many boarded ships that were captained by slave traders, who enthusiastically sold the children into slavery as soon as they arrived at their destination. Thousands died from disease, exposure, and starvation on the long march across Europe to the Mediterranean Sea. Others perished at sea.

Another story, from a modern and more familiar place, offers a soul-wrenching view of personal humiliation but also the ability to rise above it. Hatsuye Egami was one of 110,000 Japanese Americans sent to internment camps during World War II. "Since yesterday we Japanese have ceased to be human beings," he wrote in his diary. "We are numbers. We are no longer Egamis, but the number 23324. A tag with that number is on every trunk, suitcase and bag. Tags, also, on our breasts." Despite such dehumanizing treatment, most internees worked hard to control their bitterness. They created workable communities inside the camps and demonstrated again and again their loyalty as Americans.

These are but two of the many stories from history that can be found in the pages of the Lucent Books World History series. All World History titles rely on sound research and verifiable evidence, and all give students a clear sense of time, place, and chronology through maps and timelines as well as text.

All titles include a wide range of authoritative perspectives that demonstrate the complexity of historical interpretation and sharpen the reader's critical thinking skills. Formally documented quotations and annotated bibliographies enable students to locate and evaluate sources, often instantaneously via the Internet, and serve as valuable tools for further research and debate.

Finally, Lucent's World History titles present rousing good stories, featuring vivid primary source quotations drawn from unique, sometimes obscure sources such as diaries, public records, and contemporary chronicles. In this way, the voices of participants and witnesses as well as important biographers and historians bring the study of history to life. As we are caught up in the lives of others, we are reminded that we too are characters in the ongoing human saga, and we are better prepared for our own roles.

Important Dates at the Time

412 B.C.
Greek philosopher and physician Hippocrates writes of a disease characterized by cough followed by pneumonia that spreads throughout Greece.

1347
A pandemic of bubonic plague, later called the Black Death, begins to devastate Europe.

1492
Christopher Columbus arrives at the Caribbean island later named Hispaniola. The next year, influenza sweeps through the native population, killing thousands.

| 412 B.C. | 1350 | 1400 | 1450 | 1500 | 1550 | 1600 |

1357
The term *influenza* is coined from the Italian word for "influence," reflecting the belief in the influence of the stars on human events and health.

1512
Polish astronomer Copernicus advances the idea that the sun, not the earth, is the center of the solar system.

1580
The first documented pandemic of flu begins in North Africa.

1628
English physician William Harvey maps the circulation of blood.

1607
The first permanent English settlement in America is established at Jamestown, Virginia.

1798
English physician Edward Jenner publishes his work on smallpox vaccination.

of the Influenza Pandemics

1918
The Great "Spanish Flu" Pandemic of 1918 begins, eventually killing 20 million to 100 million people worldwide.

1929
The Great Depression begins.

1944
American physician Thomas Francis Jr. develops the first killed-virus flu vaccine.

1816
French physician René Laënnec invents the stethoscope

1933
British doctors isolate the first human flu virus.

1957
The "Asian flu" pandemic kills 1 million people.

| 1650 | 1700 | 1750 | 1800 | 1850 | 1900 | 1950 | 2000 | 2010 |

1968
The "Hong Kong" flu kills 34,000 Americans in the last flu pandemic of the twentieth century.

2003–2005
An epidemic of avian flu kills millions of chickens, ducks, and wild birds throughout Asia and eastern Europe.

1997
One-and-a-half million chickens are slaughtered in Hong Kong when a new strain of bird flu kills 6 people.

2009
A new strain of flu, called the H1N1 flu, sickens people in Mexico before spreading worldwide.

2010
In January WHO estimates that since April 2009, H1N1 is responsible for about 13,600 deaths worldwide.

Not Just a Bad Cold

The sickness that is today called influenza, or flu, has been tormenting mankind for thousands of years. In the fourth century B.C., about twenty-five hundred years ago, the Greek philosopher and physician Hippocrates, known as the Father of Medicine, wrote of a flulike illness that is today referred to as the Cough of Perinthus. Widespread outbreaks of flu, called epidemics, break out among the human population every year, usually in the fall, killing tens of thousands of people.

Influenza has also, from time to time, swept across the planet in devastating worldwide outbreaks called pandemics, which have killed millions of people. For example, the influenza pandemic of 1918–1919 is estimated to have killed more people in four months than the fourteenth-century Black Death pandemic did in four years. It killed more Americans than all the wars of the twentieth century. Today influenza remains a threat, as new versions, or strains, of the virus appear each flu season. Each new strain has the potential to cause a pandemic, and health officials around the globe keep a very close watch on each new outbreak.

More than a Bad Cold

In her book *Secret Agents: The Menace of Emerging Infections*, author Madeline Drexler asserts that one of the reasons influenza is so dangerous is that people tend to think of it as just a bad cold. She writes,

> Flu is the illness many public health experts dread most, because it is the only disease that results in what [scientists] call "excess mortality." The seasonal spike it brings in the death rate comes not only from influenza and pneumonia, but also from more cardiac failure and pulmonary (lung)

disease and diabetic complications than in flu-free times. . . . And by constantly changing, the flu virus mocks our annual attempt to protect ourselves with vaccination. It may be the cleverest, most agile microorganism known.[1]

Influenza is unlike most other infectious, or spreadable, illnesses because the virus that causes it can change its own genetic structure in a matter of weeks. It can also take genetic material from other viruses, add it to its own, and completely change its characteristics so that it becomes a brand-new version of itself. Flu is "a wily adversary," says Robert G. Webster, a virus expert who has studied the flu virus for over forty years. "Just when you start to think that you've understood what it can do, [it changes]. It's one of the most crafty of all infectious disease agents. It's got such a repertoire [collection] of tricks."[2]

Human Society and Influenza

Every year influenza takes an enormous toll in human life. According to the Centers for Disease Control and Prevention

This computer illustration of the influenza virus shows the center core with genetic material, the capsid surrounding the genetic core (in blue), and the lipid envelope on the outside with antigen spikes on the capsid (blue circles) that allow the virus to attach to a host cell.

(CDC) in Atlanta, Georgia, 5 to 20 percent of the population in the United States gets flu each year. Over two hundred thousand people are hospitalized from flu complications each year, and about thirty-six thousand people are estimated to die each year as a result of flu. It is one of the top-ten causes of death in the United States.

According to the World Health Organization (WHO), every year approximately 5 to 15 percent of the world's population becomes ill with respiratory system infections such as influenza. It is estimated that between a quarter and a half a million people in the world die each year from influenza. The great majority of flu deaths occur in the elderly, the very young, pregnant women, and people with other chronic health problems, especially heart and lung disease.

The economic impact of the disease also has a major impact on human society. Every year the flu causes millions of dollars in lost productivity because employees cannot go to work either because they are ill or because they must care for ill family members. Governments spend billions of dollars planning and preparing for potential epidemics and pandemics. They prepare and distribute vaccines, educate the public, maintain and update pandemic preparedness plans, and support research on the flu virus. Billions more are spent on health care related to flu, such as medications and the care of hospitalized flu patients. Every year influenza closes schools, overloads hospitals and doctors' offices, cripples transportation services, and causes significant loss of life.

Fighting Back

The influenza virus changes itself constantly, becoming an almost entirely new organism every year. It is a never-ending struggle for the world's scientists and health officials to stay ahead of the flu. Massive vaccination programs and public education efforts are conducted each year in an attempt to control outbreaks and to keep people informed about how to protect themselves and their families from getting sick. Thousands of research studies are done every year around the globe to learn more about this illness and how best to fight back.

Chapter One

What Is Influenza?

Influenza, most often referred to as "the flu," is an illness of the respiratory system—the nose, throat, trachea (windpipe), and lungs. Flu can affect birds and some mammals as well as humans. Flu is an infectious disease, which means that it can easily be spread from person to person or from animal to animal. Some types can be spread from animals to humans, and others affect only humans. Flu is most common during the fall and winter months—the "flu season"—because the virus is more stable and is more easily spread in air that is cool and dry. Each year during the flu season, flu appears in many places around the world in outbreaks called epidemics. Yearly epidemics of seasonal flu cause tens of thousands of deaths each year.

Occasionally, a new variety, or strain, of influenza appears that is especially virulent, meaning it spreads very rapidly and causes severe symptoms. This can lead to a pandemic—an especially widespread, worldwide outbreak of the disease. Flu pandemics have occurred several times throughout history. Until the development of effective ways to prevent and treat the disease, pandemic influenza caused millions of human deaths—quite an accomplishment for an organism so small that many scientists do not even consider it a living thing.

Organisms on the Edge of Life

Influenza is caused by a virus, an extremely small, disease-causing infectious agent. The words *virus* and *virulent* come from the Latin word for "poison." Other diseases caused by viruses include the common cold, smallpox, rabies, polio, measles, and mumps. Since the first virus was discovered in 1898, over five thousand different viruses have been identified. Viruses are very different from other infectious organisms, such as bacteria.

Where Do Viruses Come From?

Because viruses do not make fossils, it is hard to know how long they have actually been around. There are several theories about how viruses first came into existence.

The regressive theory says that viruses may once have been small cells that lived as parasites on larger organisms, such as bacteria. Over time, they lost whatever genetic material they did not need until they became totally dependent upon other organisms for their survival.

The second theory, called the cellular origin theory or escape theory, says that viruses may have arisen from fragments of DNA or RNA that "escaped" from other organisms. The escaped genetic material could have been particles of DNA called plasmids, which can move between cells, or it could be from transposons, segments of the DNA molecule that can replicate themselves and move into different positions along a gene.

The third theory, the coeevolution theory, states that viruslike molecules appeared at the same time that other early molecules first appeared, but instead of being collected into more complex cellular organisms, early virus particles simply became parasites on the more evolved cells. Some of them even depended on the presence of other viruses in the host cell for their survival. The hepatitis delta virus is an example; it depends on the hepatitis B virus to make its protein coat.

Bacteria are cellular organisms, with a complex internal structure. They use oxygen to create energy and can reproduce themselves. Viruses do none of that. They are not cells, and they cannot live or reproduce on their own but must invade living cells in order to function. For these reasons, many scientists do not even consider viruses to be true living organisms at all.

Also unlike bacteria, viruses are very simple structures. Most are about one-tenth the size of the average bacterium, and many are even smaller. They are so small that they cannot be seen with a regular light microscope. In fact, some types, called bacteriophages, are small enough to infect and kill bacteria. Viruses can be round or rod shaped, or they can have multiple "heads" or "tails." Viruses are made up of three main parts. First, in their center, or core, all viruses contain genetic material—a set of genes that contain the instructions for how the virus is built and how it functions. This is similar to the way a computer code determines how a computer will function and what types of programs it can run. In some viruses, such as smallpox, the genes are made of a chemical called deoxyribonucleic acid, or DNA, which is also what human genes are made of. In others, such as the flu virus, the genetic chemical is ribonucleic acid, or RNA. The flu virus has only eight genes in its core.

The second part of viruses is a covering called a capsid, which surrounds the genetic core and protects the genes. The capsid is made of protein molecules—long organic molecules essential for the functioning of all living plant and animal cells. Third, most viruses (including the flu virus) build a fatlike layer of material over the capsid called the lipid envelope, which surrounds them while they are outside of a cell. Viruses are so simple in structure that biologist Peter Medawar describes viruses as "a piece of bad news wrapped in protein."[3]

Viruses have only one job—to replicate, or reproduce themselves. Because viruses are not cells and cannot replicate themselves by dividing, as true cells do, they cannot exist for very long by themselves. Instead, they must invade the cells of an animal or human and take them over. A cell that has been invaded by a virus is called a host cell. The entire virus may enter a host cell, or it may simply inject its genetic material into a cell. Either way, once inside, the virus takes control of the structures and metabolism of the host cell. The virus genes instruct the host cell to use its own cell functions to manufacture new copies of the virus inside the host cell, similar to the way in which a computer virus takes over the workings of the computer and causes it to malfunction. A single invading virus can make the host cell produce hundreds of thousands of copies of the virus. The host cell eventually dies and breaks open, releasing all the new viruses so they can infect other cells. As the new viruses leave the host cell, they construct their lipid envelope from the broken outer membrane of the dead host cell. The influenza virus is extremely skilled at the whole process of invasion and replication.

A Constant Evolution

During the process of replication, mutations, or changes, in the virus's genetic material often occur. These changes alter the way the virus behaves and responds to its host's immune system. This process of change, called antigenic drift, creates new strains of the virus that are somewhat different from the previous strains, but still genetically similar. A second way in which viruses can change into new strains is by picking up pieces of RNA or DNA from other strains of flu that may already be in the animal they infect, a process called reassortment or antigenic shift. Reassortment happens much less frequently than antigenic drift. Viruses can also reassort by taking pieces of the infected animal's own genetic material before replicating. Unlike antigenic drift, reassortment can change as much as one-third of the virus's genetic makeup, resulting in versions of the virus that are completely unlike the previous strains. Virus expert Robert G. Webster says, "If antigenic drift were compared to a shudder, antigenic shift would be likened to an earthquake."[4]

Viruses with DNA at their core have an internal mechanism that keeps mutations and antigenic drift to a minimum as they replicate. RNA viruses, however, are much more prone to mutating, so RNA viruses, such as the influenza virus, are particularly good at both antigenic drift and reassortment. The flu virus's tendency to mutate when it replicates is also the feature that allows it to survive by changing its genetic nature so frequently. "The paradox is that this is apparently a very fragile virus," says flu researcher Edwin Kilbourne. "Unless it mutates, it's going to disappear. It's an ephemeral [lasting a very short time] virus, with remarkable tenacity [stubbornness] and adaptability."[5]

The Influenza Virus

The virus that causes the flu is a member of a group of viruses with the name Orthomyxoviridae. There are three main types of influenza viruses—influenza A, influenza B, and influenza C. Influenza A is the most virulent of the three. It can mutate very quickly, and there are many different genetic variations, or subtypes, of influenza A. Each subtype may have any number of strains, depending on how the subtype has mutated that particular year. Influenza A is the kind of flu that affects humans most often, but it did not originate in humans. It began in birds.

Domestic fowl, such as chickens and turkeys, and wild water birds, such as geese and ducks, naturally carry many strains of influenza A in their intestinal tract. In birds, the disease is called avian influenza. Wild birds rarely get sick from avian flu, but domestic birds can get sick and die from it. Other mammals, especially pigs, can also carry flu in their bodies. In pigs, the illness is called swine flu. Most flu in humans is caused by avian strains of influenza A, but avian flu does not normally infect humans all by itself. It must first become adapted to human cells before it can make people sick. This adaptation happens in a process that Webster calls the "barnyard theory."

When bird droppings from infected birds enter water sources, the virus can be spread to other animals, such as pigs, which drink the contaminated water. Pigs can carry both human and avian strains of flu in their bodies as well as their own swine flu strains. In the body of the pig, the avian virus is able to combine its genes with human and swine flu genes—the process of antigenic shift. In this way, an entirely new flu virus is created that has never circulated among humans before.

When the human body is exposed to a virus, the immune system immediately creates chemicals called antibodies which fight the infection. If the person is later exposed to the same virus, he or she will have built-up immunity to that virus and will not get sick from it. If a person is exposed to a new strain, however, the antibodies cannot recognize it and there is no immunity to it. The new strain can spread extremely rapidly between people and make it around the world in just

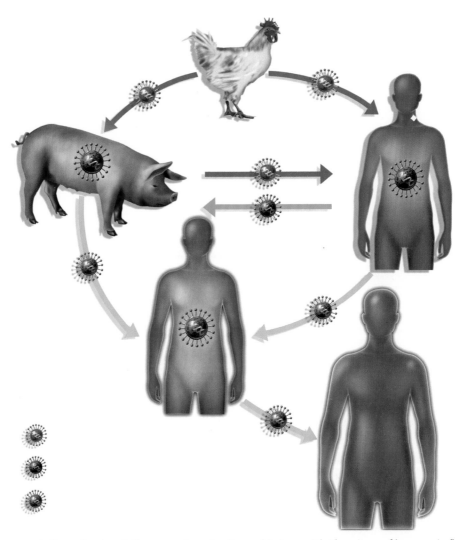

A representation of avian influenza virus (red) combining with the virus of human influenza (green), resulting in a new mutant virus that is highly contagious and deadly to people (blue).

a few weeks. This is how influenza A causes pandemics. Any place in which humans, pigs, and fowl live closely together is a possible starting place for a pandemic.

Influenza B is almost exclusively a disease of humans. Its symptoms are milder than those of influenza A, and it does not cause pandemics because it rarely goes through reassortment and mutates much slower. Influenza C can infect humans, pigs, and dogs, but it is much less common than the other types and only occasionally causes mild illness in children.

It also does not cause pandemics. Influenza B and C are not classified into subtypes.

Influenza A Subtypes

On the outer surface of the flu virus are two kinds of protein particles, called hemagglutinin (HA) and neuraminidase (NA). HA allows the virus to bind to the host cell and release its RNA into the cell. NA controls the release of the newly made viruses out of the infected cell. HA and NA are antigens, which means that they trigger the human immune system to respond to the presence of the virus by making antibodies. There are fifteen known types of HA antigens and nine types of NA antigens found on influenza A viruses.

Influenza A subtypes are named according to which type of HA and NA antigens are present on the surface of the virus. The subtypes are given two letters—H for hemagglutinin, and N for neuraminidase—and two numbers that designate which form of HA and NA the virus has. The most well-known influenza A subtypes are H1N1, a type of swine flu; H2N2, which caused a flu pandemic in 1957; H3N2, which caused a pandemic in 1968; and H5N1, an avian strain which can cause severe symptoms in humans but is not easily spread from person to person.

Symptoms and Complications of Influenza

The influenza virus is not the same virus that causes the common cold, even though many of the symptoms may be similar in the early stages of the disease. Influenza symptoms can begin very suddenly—sometimes within hours of exposure to the virus. The first sign is usually a moderate to high fever of 100°F to 103°F (38°C to 39°C), along with chills and shivering. Most people with the flu feel fatigued, or extremely tired and weak, and may not get out of bed except to go to the bathroom. They may also have muscle aches throughout their bodies, especially in their back and legs. Flu may also cause a dry cough, runny nose, watery eyes, loss of appetite, and headache. Young children with influenza may also experience nausea, vomiting, and diarrhea. While the common cold usually runs its course in a couple of days, the symptoms of flu can last a week or more, with extra days needed to regain strength.

In otherwise healthy adults, flu is usually a self-limiting disease, which means it will run its course without special treatment, and recovery is complete. Sometimes, however, influenza can lead to more serious problems that may require hospitalization and can even cause death. These complications are more likely to happen in the very young or the elderly, because these groups tend to have weaker immune systems than healthy adults, and in people with other long-term health problems, such as heart or lung disease. Influenza can make these other health problems worse because the organs involved are already weakened by disease.

The most serious complication of influenza is pneumonia. Pneumonia is not actually a disease by itself. It is a complication that can result from many health problems. Pneumonia is a condition in which the lungs fill with fluids, which significantly interferes with their function. A person with pneumonia may have a worsened cough, difficulty breathing, and high fever and may possibly cough up blood. Pneumonia is most often caused by a bacterial infection that attacks the weakened immune system of the person already ill with influenza, but

Flu symptoms include chills and shivering, muscle aches, dry cough, runny nose, headache, and loss of appetite.

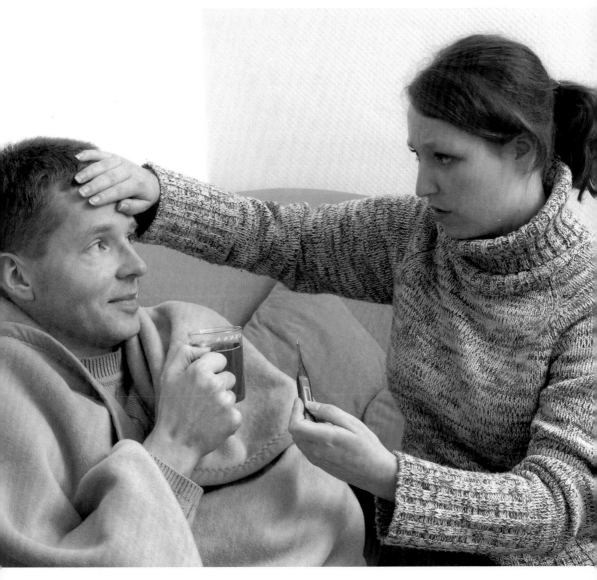

Reye's Syndrome

Reye's syndrome is a very serious, potentially fatal disease that is almost always associated with viral illnesses, especially influenza and chicken pox. It has also been connected with the use of aspirin during the course of the viral illness. It mostly affects children and teens and only rarely affects adults. For this reason, doctors caution against giving children and teens any aspirin or aspirin-like medications when they have a viral illness. Acetaminophen or ibuprofen are safe alternatives.

Reye's syndrome begins at about the time a person is recovering from a virus. The disease causes abnormally large amounts of fat to accumulate around the liver and other organs, which interferes with their function. It also causes a profound increase in pressure in the brain. The first symptoms include vomiting, loss of energy, and excessive drowsiness. These signs are followed by distinct changes in behavior, including aggressiveness, irritability, and confusion. As the pressure in the brain increases, there may be convulsions and coma. Left untreated, significant brain damage or death can occur within a few days.

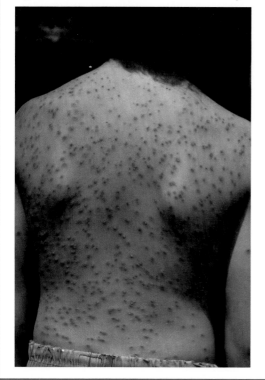

Reye's syndrome is a medical emergency, and diagnosis and treatment must take place quickly. Treatment centers on measures to protect the brain from damage caused by swelling. Some people recover completely; others may be left with brain damage. Recovery depends on prompt treatment and reducing brain swelling.

Reye's syndrome is a serious and potentially fatal disease that is almost always associated with viral illnesses such as influenza and chicken pox.

it may also be caused by the flu virus itself. When it occurs, it usually appears about five days after the onset of flu symptoms.

Children with influenza are at risk for other complications besides pneumonia, such as sinus or ear infections. More serious complications include meningitis and encephalitis, especially under age one. Meningitis is the inflammation of the membranes surrounding the brain and the spinal cord (the meninges). High fever, headache, and a stiff neck are the most common symptoms. Encephalitis is an inflammation of the brain itself as well as the membranes that surround it, causing swelling and irritation. It can cause headaches, seizures, drowsiness, confusion, loss of consciousness, bleeding in the brain, and damage to the brain if not treated quickly. If these complications are caused by a bacterial infection, they are treated with antibiotics. Other drugs to control swelling and prevent seizures may also be given.

How Influenza Causes Illness

Different strains of influenza can cause different symptoms, with some being quite mild and others being more severe. Symptoms are caused by the damage that the virus does to the tissues they infect. The difference lies in the genetic makeup of each individual strain and the structure of the HA protein on its surface.

The HA protein, which allows the virus to invade the host cell, also determines what parts of the body will be most affected by that particular strain. For example, milder forms of flu may only invade cells that are found in the nose and throat. This means that they only infect cells and cause symptoms in those areas. Other flu strains, such as the dangerous H5N1 subtype, can invade cells much deeper in the lungs and in other parts of the body, such as the intestinal tract, causing more severe symptoms.

Some of the classic symptoms of flu are caused not by the virus itself but by the body's normal immune response to a foreign invader. Fever, headache, chills, fatigue, and body aches are all signs that the immune system has recognized an invading organism and has kicked in to fight it. One particular type of immune response, however, can cause death as easily and as quickly as the illness it was meant to fight—the cytokine storm.

Cytokine Storm

Cytokine storm is a dangerous and potentially fatal event that can happen during the flu and other illnesses. When the human immune system is triggered by an infectious agent, such as the flu virus, chemicals called cytokines are produced by immune system cells called leukocytes, or white blood cells. Cytokines are signaling molecules; they signal other kinds of immune system cells to travel to the site of the infection. Cytokines also signal those immune system cells to produce more cytokines. This immune response causes inflammation, which is seen when the body temperature goes up or when tissues

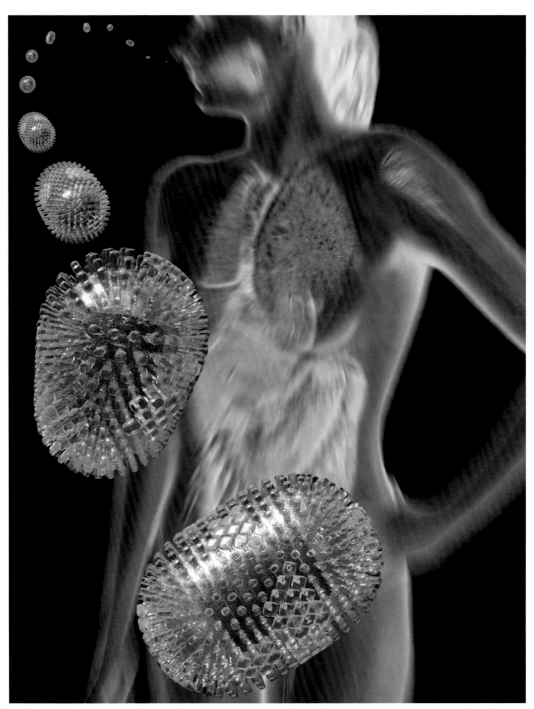

This illustration shows a cytokine storm reaction to avian influenza. Avian flu viruses (green) are inhaled and enter the lungs (olive green). The virus induces an immune system cytokine storm that inflames the airways, leading to breathing difficulties and fatal respiratory distress.

swell. Normally, this cycle between cytokines and immune system cells, and the inflammation it causes, are kept under control.

Sometimes, though, in the presence of an especially virulent infection, or if the pathogen is something the body has never seen before, the cytokine cycle can spin out of control. When this happens, far too many immune cells are sent to the infection site and too much cytokine is produced. This is a cytokine storm. Cytokine storms can do a great deal of damage to whatever part of the body they occur in. For example, if a cytokine storm occurs in the lungs, then the inflammatory response it sets off causes the lungs to fill with fluid, causing a severe pneumonia and the airways to become blocked. Cytokine storms can actually cause the death of the human or animal in which they happen.

Another possibly harmful consequence of the cytokine response is that it can be focused so much on attacking the flu virus that it leaves the body vulnerable to other infections, such as bacterial pneumonia. Physician Jan Gurley says,

Unfortunately, the unintended consequence of your body's eager flu reaction is that it can leave you very susceptible to bacterial infections. Kind of like rushing all your body's troops off to battle invaders on the Western front, while leaving your Eastern territory completely unguarded. In practical terms, this means that you have to keep watch, even after flu symptoms seem to get better. A new fever, a worse cough, a sudden bad headache, a strange rash—all of these can mean wicked bacteria have invaded and are running relatively unchecked while your body is still focused on the flu. Sometimes it's only after a normally healthy person gets overwhelmingly sick with a bacterial infection that healthcare providers realize a prior flu infection might be part of the problem.[6]

Diagnosis of Influenza

In the very young, the elderly, and in people with other health problems, flu can cause serious complications, such as pneumonia and cytokine storm. It can and does cause many thousands of deaths every year. There are drugs that are effective at treating flu by shortening the duration of the illness, reducing the severity of the symptoms, and minimizing the risk of complications, but they are most effective when they are started early on in the disease. Diagnosing influenza quickly and accurately is very important.

Usually the diagnosis can be made based just on the pattern of symptoms. Fever, fatigue, body aches, and dry cough are usually enough to diagnose the flu. Laboratory tests can be used to confirm the diagnosis as well as to determine the particular strain of flu involved. This is especially important for people who are at risk for complications. Lab tests for flu are useful if there is an outbreak of a respiratory disease in a community and the cause is unknown. Because of the time and expense involved, the Centers for Disease Control and Prevention (CDC) in Atlanta, Georgia, recommends that lab testing be done on ill people only until the presence of flu in the community is confirmed, and then only for those who develop more severe symptoms or who are at high risk for complications.

Rapid flu tests are simple tests that can be done in a doctor's office. A swab of the nose or throat is taken and tested for the presence of viruses. They take ten to thirty minutes to complete, so they are quick, but they are not always accurate, and they cannot distinguish between different strains of flu. Another method is a viral culture, in which material from the nose or throat is added to a special growing material called a culture medium that contains cells that the virus can infect. The culture medium is then examined for growth of viruses. Cultures are much more accurate and can provide information about the type of strain that is present, but they can take up to ten days to complete.

Transmission of Influenza

Influenza can spread from person to person in three ways. The most direct way is when a person with flu coughs or sneezes close to another person and the virus-laden droplets get directly in the other person's eyes, nose, or mouth. A person can also pick up the virus by breathing in tiny droplets that have been coughed or sneezed into the air and are not heavy enough to land on the ground. A third way is through contact with objects that an ill person has handled or by direct contact with the infected person. Flu viruses can survive for about five minutes on skin and up to two days on hard surfaces, such as doorknobs, telephones, or stair handrails.

When a person is able to spread the flu to others, he or she is said to be "shedding virus." People with the flu shed the most virus on the second or third day after infection. Because of their weaker immune systems, children shed more virus and can spread the flu from before they even show symptoms until up to two weeks after infection. This is why flu epidemics tend to worsen early in the fall, when children return to school, spread the virus to each other, and carry it home.

Some strains of flu do not spread as easily as others. Besides determining how well the flu virus gets into a cell and the severity of the symptoms, the HA antigen also determines how easily the virus can spread from person to person. Those strains that infect mainly the upper respiratory tract—the nose, throat, and mouth—are easily spread when a person coughs or sneezes. Strains that target cells deeper in the lungs are more dangerous to the person infected, but are not as easily transmitted to other people.

Treatment of Influenza

Treating influenza mainly involves treating the symptoms of the disease. People with the flu can help themselves recover by getting plenty of rest,

Influenza can easily spread from person to person via airborne germs that are emitted when an ill person sneezes or coughs and another inhales the droplets in the air.

The Pandemic Severity Index

The Pandemic Severity Index (PSI) is a way to classify influenza pandemics according to their predicted severity. It was developed by the Centers for Disease Control and Prevention (CDC) in Atlanta, Georgia, and released by the U.S. Department of Health and Human Services on February 1, 2007. It includes a set of guidelines that help states, communities, businesses, and schools decide what kinds of measures need to be taken to slow the spread of a flu pandemic in case vaccines and antiviral drugs are in short supply. Such measures include isolating and treating ill people, voluntary quarantine of people who have been in contact with ill people, closing schools, and canceling events that might draw large crowds.

The main factors used to decide the severity of a pandemic include how likely the disease is to spread worldwide; what measures are already in place to slow it down; and the case-fatality ratio (CFR), the number of deaths that occur compared to the total number of cases reported. The PSI categorizes a potential pandemic as a number from one to five, with five being the most severe. The Spanish flu pandemic of 1918, which killed hundreds of millions, was designated a category five, while regular seasonal flu is usually a category one. The H1N1 pandemic of 2009 was a category two, largely because an effective vaccine was made widely available in time to prevent more spread of the disease.

drinking lots of fluids, and not using tobacco or drinking alcohol. For the fever and body aches, over-the-counter anti-inflammatory medications, such as acetaminophen and ibuprofen, are helpful. Children and teens should never take aspirin when they have the flu because there is a chance of developing a serious complication called Reye's syndrome. Usually influenza runs its course naturally in about a week.

With the development of antibiotic drugs, such as penicillin, in the late 1930s and early 1940s, pneumonia, which may complicate the flu, can be treated, saving thousands of lives. But antibiotics are only effective against bacterial infections. They are useless against viral infections, and they are not used to treat the flu unless there is an overlying bacterial infection such as pneumonia.

In 1966 a new class of drugs called adamantanes, also called M2 inhibitors, was introduced. Drugs in this class include amantadine and rimantadine. Adamantanes slow the progression of flu by blocking a flu protein called M2, which allows the virus to "uncoat" its protein capsid once inside the host cell.

Without this ability, the virus cannot introduce its genetic material into the host cell and therefore cannot replicate itself. Adamantanes helped to prevent the onset of flu symptoms after exposure to the virus and lessened the severity of the symptoms after they had already begun. It also shortened the length of time needed to recover from the flu. Today adamantanes are no longer widely used to treat flu because the virus has developed a resistance to them.

Another class of antiviral medications, called neuraminidase inhibitors, or NA inhibitors, was developed in 1996. Drugs in this class include Tamiflu and Relenza. NA inhibitors block the action of the NA antigen on the surface of the virus so that new viruses cannot get out of the host cell to infect other cells.

Prevention

The simplest way to prevent getting the flu is to minimize contact with the virus. The most effective way to do this is to observe good hygiene habits, especially hand washing with soap and water or with alcohol-based hand sanitizers. Other ways to avoid getting the flu are by not touching the eyes, nose, and mouth any more than necessary and by staying away from ill people. The best ways to avoid spreading the flu to others are to observe good hand washing, stay home from work or school, and cover coughs and sneezes. Disinfecting surfaces with rubbing alcohol or a dilute bleach solution kills the virus and can also help minimize its transmission.

When community outbreaks occur, public health officials take actions to minimize the number of people who get sick. They provide information about the flu to the community to educate people about ways to avoid getting it and about the symptoms. Schools, churches, and other places where groups of people gather may choose to close until the threat has subsided, but there is little evidence to suggest that this actually reduces transmission. All these measures are very valuable in controlling the spread of flu, but the most effective way to avoid the flu is by getting vaccinated each year.

Vaccination

Vaccination is a very effective way to avoid contracting an illness such as flu and to minimize the spread of the disease. A vaccine is an injection of a virus which as been weakened (called live attenuated vaccine) or chemically inactivated (killed vaccine) so that it can no longer cause illness. When the vaccine is injected, however, the body's immune system immediately responds as if the virus was fully active by producing antibodies to it. The antibodies made in response to the vaccine prevent the person from getting sick if he or she is exposed to the live virus. The vaccinated person may feel some symptoms of the immune response, such as a mild fever, but is not actually getting sick.

Because the flu virus changes itself so rapidly, the flu vaccine must also be changed each year to be effective against whichever strains are predicted to appear.

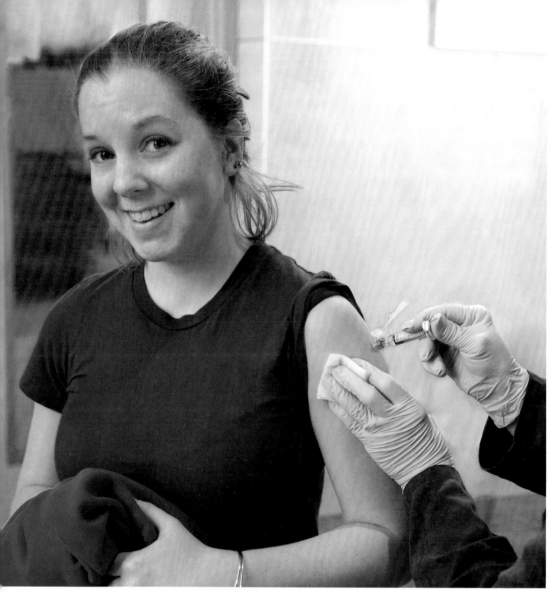

Vaccination is the most effective way to avoid contacting influenza and minimizing the spread of the disease.

Flu vaccines are formulated to be effective against several strains at once, but they take about two weeks to reach full effectiveness. A vaccinated person can still get the flu if he or she is exposed to a strain that is not included in that year's vaccine, or if the person was exposed less than two weeks before getting vaccinated. Despite this, flu vaccines are highly effective. Vaccination is especially important for those at high risk for complications.

Epidemics and Pandemics

Every year through antigenic drift, new strains of influenza appear, and every year health officials work to develop a vaccine that will be effective against that year's collection of strains. Despite their best efforts, however, epidemics happen every year in the fall and winter. Since the Northern and Southern Hemispheres have their fall and winter at different times, there are actually two flu seasons and two epidemics each year, causing an estimated five hundred thousand deaths around the world.

When reassortment creates a novel strain that is so different from previous strains that no one has immunity to it, a pandemic can occur. Flu pandemics, on average, infect about 15 to 40 percent of those who are exposed to it, but a high infection rate does not always lead to a high mortality rate. How many people die from it depends on how well the virus is able to resist the human immune system. Pandemics tend to occur in waves, with later waves often worse than earlier ones. Flu pandemics have occurred throughout history, some worse than others, but all causing thousands or even millions of deaths.

Chapter Two

Influenza in the Past

Influenza is a disease that infects not only humans but also many other mammals and birds. Flu viruses have been found in pigs, sheep, horses, ducks, chickens, and turkeys. Influenza in humans may have started when animals such as these were first domesticated and brought in close contact with humans, about six thousand years ago. Gradually their flu viruses adapted to humans and mutated into strains that could make people sick. As humans formed permanent settlements, the virus was able to spread easily from person to person, causing epidemics.

It is difficult to establish with certainty whether or not an outbreak of a disease that occurred long ago was a true pandemic, or if it was simply an epidemic that affected a large area. Diseases, their causes, and their transmission were not fully understood until the nineteenth century, so existing descriptions vary widely from writer to writer. Diseases, es-

pecially respiratory illnesses, were often attributed to "bad air" or imbalances in body fluids. In ancient times there were no formal, reliable methods for tracking the spread of a disease, and communication between different parts of the world was very slow, dependent upon written messages carried over land or by sea. According to the World Health Organization (WHO), if written descriptions indicate that an illness spread to several parts of the world and caused a lot of deaths, it can be defined as a probable pandemic. Also according to WHO, if the epidemic occurred during the warmer months of the year, it may be considered a pandemic since a simple outbreak would have subsided after the normal fall and winter season for the illness.

Because of the lack of understanding of disease in the past, it is also difficult to determine with certainty if a recorded outbreak of a respiratory illness was actually caused by influenza or any one of a number of other similar illnesses known to exist, such as diphtheria, typhoid fever, dengue, typhus, or even plague. What is known is that flu-like illnesses have been occurring since ancient times.

The Cough of Perinthus

The ancient work *Of the Epidemics*, written in the late fifth and early fourth centuries B.C., is often attributed to Hippocrates, a Greek physician and philosopher, but it is most likely a collection of observations by several physicians of the time. In Book VI, attributed to Hippocrates and his son, Thessalus, a detailed account is given of an illness bearing a striking resemblance to modern influenza. In it, the writers describe coughs that begin in the winter, accompanied by symptoms such as pneumonia, sore throat, body aches, and difficulty swallowing and breathing.

When *Of the Epidemics* was translated into French in the early 1800s, the translator attributed these symptoms to a single disease and called it an epidemic, which he named the Cough of Perinthus, for the town in western Turkey where most of the illness seemed to be happening. The word *epidemic*, however, meant something different in the time of Hippocrates than it

does now. Back then, it meant a group of illnesses seen in a particular place at a particular time, rather than a single disease seen in many people at once. Modern scholars who accept this older definition of *epidemic* consider the symptoms of the Cough of Perinthus to have

The earliest known reference to the possible symptoms of influenza are in the works of Hippocrates, a Greek physician who lived in the late fifth century B.C.

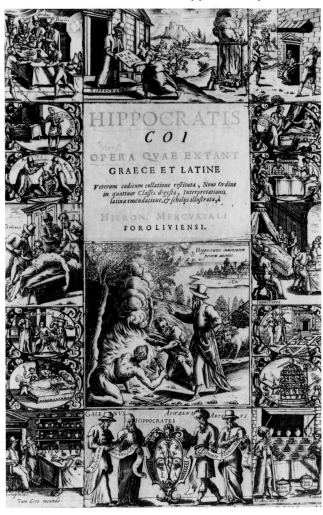

most likely represented a group of several related illnesses, such as diphtheria and whooping cough, as well as influenza, rather than an actual epidemic of a single disease.

Influenza in the Middle Ages

Several widespread outbreaks of what was possibly influenza occurred during the Middle Ages. Various historians have described several outbreaks in the ninth and tenth centuries. According to German physician and medical historian August Hirsch (1817–1894), the first epidemic that can definitely be called influenza occurred in 1173, but several others place the first true flu epidemic at later dates through the twelfth, thirteenth, and fourteenth centuries. Still other historians say that 1510 is the date of the first epidemic that can reasonably be attributed to influenza.

Many outbreaks of flulike illnesses are described throughout the centuries leading up to the twentieth century, but without the benefit of modern knowledge of infectious diseases, not all can be definitely blamed on influenza. Since the flu virus changes so rapidly and can look different from year to year, it is almost impossible to say with any certainty if a particular illness was really influenza, or any one of a number of similar diseases.

The Sweating Sickness

In late August 1485 Henry VII of England, fresh from his defeat of Richard III in the Battle of Bosworth, arrived in London to begin his reign as king. His coronation had to be postponed, however, because of a mysterious illness that had begun to sweep through the capital city. London's physicians knew it was not the plague, the devastating and deadly disease which had almost destroyed Europe the previous century, but neither was it like any other disease they had seen before.

Symptoms began very suddenly, with a vague feeling of anxiety followed by fever with shaking chills, headache, extreme fatigue, abdominal pain, severe shortness of breath, and severe pains in the neck, back, and shoulders. These symptoms would last several hours, after which a new set of symptoms would set in, including delirium, rapid heartbeat, and the sweating that gave the illness its name. Polydore Virgil, a writer of the time, recorded a vivid description of the disease. He writes,

> A sudden deadly sweating attacked the body, and at the same time, head and stomach were in pain from the violence of the fever. When seized by the disease, some were unable to bear the heat, and, if in bed, removed their bedclothes, or, if clothed, undressed themselves; others slaked [quenched] their thirst with cold drinks, yet others endured the heat and the stench (for the perspiration stank foully). . . . But all alike died, either as soon as the fever began or not long after, so that of all the persons infected,

barely one in a hundred escaped death. And those who survived twenty-four hours after the sweating ended . . . were not free of it, since they continually relapsed and many perished thereafter.[7]

When the sweating sickness swept London in 1602 its most notable casualty was Henry VIII's brother, Arthur, Prince of Wales.

Death could occur within hours of the first symptoms, and people were literally dying in the streets. Physicians could do little for their patients except to put them to bed and try to alleviate the symptoms. Families were told not to let their ill ones sleep, because it was thought that this would lead to death.

By the end of October, when the disease finally began to subside, it had killed several thousand people, rich and poor alike, including London's lord mayor and six aldermen (councilmen) of the city. A similar illness struck Ireland in 1492, but it is not known if it was actually the same disease. In 1502 the sweating sickness claimed the life of Arthur, prince of Wales, the older brother of Henry VIII. Henry later married Arthur's young bride, Catherine—the first of his six wives.

The sweating sickness returned to England in 1507 and again in 1517. The 1517 outbreak was a bad one, and in some towns almost half the population died from it. A fourth outbreak came in 1528 and quickly spread throughout England. Henry VIII, now king, left London to escape it, changing his residence as much as every two days to avoid it. This time, the illness spread throughout Europe, causing thousands of deaths, although there is no record of it ever striking France or Italy. By the end of the year, it had almost

Medicine in the Middle Ages

Physicians in the Middle Ages (the fifth through the fifteenth centuries) could do little to help people with influenza. Medical thought at the time was still based on ancient Greek and Roman teaching. One belief was that illness was caused by an imbalance of fluids in the body, which were called the "humors"—black bile, yellow bile, phlegm, and blood. Any imbalance in one of the humors could cause disease in the part of the body where the humor was made. Illness was also blamed on evil spirits, superstition, astrological signs, magic, or divine punishment for sinful ways. Dissection of human bodies was forbidden, so little was known about internal anatomy.

Besides physicians, who were trained in the prevailing medical thought of the day, untrained practitioners, such as barbers, midwives, medicine women, and faith healers, also treated illnesses and injuries. Treatment of illness mostly centered on restoring the balance of the humors and on folk remedies using herbs and medicinal plants. Humoral balance could be achieved by purging with laxatives or sweating in a hot bath. Bloodletting, in which a vein was opened and blood allowed to flow out, was very common and remained in use even into the late nineteenth century. Respiratory illnesses, such as influenza, might be treated with a medicine made from licorice and an herb called comfrey, or with a plant called lungwort. Medical thought and practice remained basically unchanged until the Renaissance of the fifteenth century.

This medieval drawing depicts a doctor bleeding a patient's arm and collecting the "bad blood" in a vessel.

completely disappeared. A fifth outbreak occurred in 1551 and, after a very brief reappearance in England in 1578, it never came back again.

The true cause of the sweating sickness has never been determined. Because of the symptoms and the highly contagious nature of the disease, a highly virulent strain of influenza has been considered as one possible cause. However, unlike typical influenza, it especially killed young, healthy men. Women, the very young, and the very old were mostly spared. For this reason, other possible illnesses, such as hantavirus, have also been offered as possible causes of the sweating sickness. It is thought that the illness was brought to England by Frenchmen who had accompanied Henry VII in his fight for the English crown. The French soldiers were mostly immune to the disease, but the English, having never been exposed to this illness before, were highly susceptible to it.

One physician of the time, named John Caius, wrote about the sweating sickness in 1552. He describes the rapidity with which the disease could kill, writing (in old English) that it

immediately killed some in opening theire windows, some in plaieng with children in their strete dores, some in one hour, many in two it destroyed, &. . . to the that merilye dined, it gave a sorowful Supper. As it founde them, so it toke them, some in sleape some in wake, some in mirthe some in care, some fast-ing and some ful, some busy and some idle, and in one house somet-yme three sometyme five, sometyme seven sometyme eight, sometyme more, sometime all.[8]

Caius suggests the cause of the disease to be a combination of several things, including the influence of the constellations, "whiche hath a great power & dominion in al erthly thinges," the corrupt and infecting nature of the soil and air in England, and the "impure spirites" in the bodies of the people, caused by eating too much bad meat and rotten fruit.

Influenza Comes to the Americas

It is not known for sure how many people were living in the Caribbean islands when the first Europeans, led by Italian explorer Christopher Columbus, arrived in 1492, but the population is estimated at anywhere from 250,000 to over 1 million. It is known, however, that after Columbus's second visit to the island of Santo Domingo in 1493, symptoms of what is thought to be influenza appeared very suddenly and swept through the native Arawak population. It eventually killed thousands of Arawak, along with about twelve hundred Spanish sailors. Bartolomé de Las Casas, a Catholic bishop, wrote extensively about the depopulation of the islands. "Hispaniola is depopulated, robbed and destroyed," he wrote in 1516. "Because in just four months, one third of the Indians . . . have died."[9] In 1552 he wrote,

Columbus's arrival in Hispaniola in 1493 brought with it an influenza epidemic that wiped out two thirds of the native population.

On Saturday 29 March [1494], the Admiral [Columbus] arrived at La Isabela and found the people of La Isabela were in sad condition because few of them had escaped being sick or dying. . . . Don Bartholomew Columbus [Columbus's brother] in arriving in Isabela found that almost 300 [Spaniards] had died of different diseases. Witnessing the plight of the Indian every day was even worse. There was so much disease, death, and misery, that innumerable fathers, mothers, and children died. . . . Of the multitudes on this island in the year 1494, by 1506, it was thought that there were but one third of all of them left.[10]

Columbus himself also became ill during this epidemic and did not fully recover until the following March.

Because of the sudden onset of the illness in late autumn, its symptoms, rapid spread, and high mortality rate, and the fact that eight pigs brought along on the voyage were allowed to freely interbreed with wild swine on the island, historians suspect that the illness that ravaged the native population may have been a strain of swine flu. Because of influenza and other European diseases, such as smallpox and typhus, by 1517 there were only about fourteen thousand Arawak left in Hispaniola. A census taken in 1574 does not mention any Arawak natives at all—only Spaniards and the African slaves they had imported to replace the decimated native population.

Influenza During the Age of Discovery

The arrival of Europeans in the New World sparked a period of intense exploration and mapping of the world known as the age of discovery, or the age of exploration. During the sixteenth and seventeenth centuries, sailors from Spain, Portugal, England, France, and the Netherlands set out on numerous expeditions around the world to find new trading partners and new routes to the East Indies and its gold, silver, silk, and precious spices. One consequence of world exploration was that the sailors on the ships carried European illnesses, such as typhus, smallpox, and influenza, around the globe. In 1510 a pandemic of a respiratory illness, now thought to be influenza because of its rapid spread, began in Africa, and, according to a writer of the time, "attacked at once and raged all over Europe not missing a family and scarce a person."[11]

The first truly global pandemic that most historians agree was actually influenza occurred in 1580. It began in Asia during the summer and quickly spread from port to port across northern Africa. From there, it spread to Italy, up the Italian peninsula, and into southern Europe, where it is estimated to have struck almost 80 percent of the population. In Rome alone, about eight thousand people died. Following trade and military routes, it went around the Mediterranean to Spain, where whole towns were depopulated, and up into western Europe. From there, it spread westward across the English Channel and through the British Isles during the late summer and into the fall. It also went eastward, throughout the rest of Europe. By November it had gotten as far north as Sweden. From Europe the flu was carried across the Atlantic to the Americas and the Caribbean, where almost 90 percent of the population was affected.

The seventeenth century was also a time of great political, economic, and military expansion between Europe and Africa, Asia, and the Americas. Greatly expanded world travel during this time meant more contact between people in more parts of the world. As a result, significant epidemics of influenza occurred throughout the century, especially in 1627–1628, 1647, 1657–1658, 1675, 1688, and 1693. In 1699 prominent Puritan minister Cotton Mather wrote, "The sickness extended to allmost all families. Few or none escaped, and many dyed especially in Boston, and some dyed in a strange or unusual manner, in some families all weer sick together, in some towns almost all weer sick so that it was a time of disease."[12]

Flu in the Eighteenth and Nineteenth Centuries

There were at least three influenza pandemics during the eighteenth century. The early years of the century saw several outbreaks in France, Denmark, Germany, and Italy, but in the spring of 1729, an especially virulent pandemic outbreak began that seemed to come from Russia. Although there is no written documentation that the pandemic actually began in Russia, there are reports from early 1729 of outbreaks in two Russian cities—Moscow and Astrakhan. The illness showed up in Sweden in September and in Austria in October. Hungary, Poland, Germany, England, and Ireland were hit in November. Although thousands were sickened by this flu, deaths were relatively low, with most occurring in northern Italy and among pregnant women and the elderly.

A second pandemic took place in 1732. This pandemic may have been a worsening of the earlier outbreaks, or it may have been an entirely different strain. Some researchers believe that it began in New England, in North America, and spread to Europe from there. Others believe that it more likely began in Russia, which, due to Peter the Great's desire to modernize his country, had much more contact than it had had before with western Europe. Between the fall of 1732 and January 1733, the flu sickened people throughout most of Europe, from Russia to the Atlantic Ocean and from the Mediterranean Sea north to Scotland. It also erupted in North America in 1732 and spread along the Atlantic coast from Massachusetts to Maine.

A third flu pandemic occurred in 1781–1782. This one may also have started in Russia or possibly China and quickly moved from east to west, across Europe to the Atlantic Ocean in about eight months. This pandemic was notable for its morbidity rate—the sheer numbers of people it sickened—especially young adults. Tens of millions of people, almost 75 percent of

The Age of Discovery

The period from the mid-fifteenth century to the mid-sixteenth century is called the age of discovery. During this time, European ships set sail from Portugal, Spain, Italy, England, France, and Holland, led by courageous explorers such as Christopher Columbus, Vasco da Gama, John Cabot, Prince Henry the Navigator, Vasco Núñez de Balboa, Ferdinand Magellan, and Francisco Pizarro.

Several factors motivated these voyages. One was the spice trade. Europeans had become dependent on Asian spices, such as cinnamon, nutmeg, cloves, ginger, and pepper, both for flavor and to help preserve food throughout the winter. The traditional overland routes had become controlled by Muslim tribes, so new overseas routes were needed. Another factor was religion, as Europeans sought to spread Christianity to the people they encountered on their voyages. European rulers were quick to support voyages due to a desire for new lands to control and the riches that might be found there.

Early voyages were fraught with danger and hardship. Little was known about what lay across the "Ocean Sea." Navigational instruments were simple and unreliable. Myths about sea monsters, giant whirlpools, and falling off the edge of the world created fear among sailors. Ships could be wrecked on uncharted reefs or sunk in violent storms. Starvation, dehydration, and illness were common onboard ship. Native peoples in the newly discovered lands were often hostile.

The age of discovery led to the improvement of cartography, or mapmaking; the development of better navigational tools; increased knowledge about the world and its people; and vastly increased wealth and power for the nations of Europe. These things came at a price, however, as European explorers brought poverty, disease, and loss of freedom to those they encountered.

the population of Europe, had become ill by August 1782. It had a relatively low mortality rate, however, with most deaths occurring in people who already had some kind of respiratory illness, such as tuberculosis.

In his book, *Epidemics and Pandemics: Their Impacts on Human History*, author J.N. Hays points out that the influenza pandemic of 1781–1782 influenced the ways in which Europeans understood disease. He writes, "Its evident movement against prevailing west-to-east winds argued that perhaps this (and other or all diseases) was carried by contagion from person to person, not by

Pandemics and Asia

Several of the more significant influenza pandemics in history seem to have begun in Asia or in areas with similar environments. The reason for this is reassortment—the ability of the influenza virus to pick up pieces of RNA from the animals it infects and thereby change its genetic makeup to become an entirely different strain.

The two major reservoirs for the influenza virus are humans and fowl, such as ducks and chickens. Human strains generally do not spread among birds, and bird strains do not normally spread to humans. Pigs, however, can carry both avian and human strains in their bodies, as well as their own swine strains. Pigs can act as "mixing bowls" for influenza viruses. In other words, while human and avian strains rarely mix with each other, they can both mix with swine strains. Through antigenic shift, an avian strain can pick up human flu genes while in a pig and become a brand-new strain able to infect humans. From this, a pandemic can start. In a 1994 article for the *European Journal of Epidemiology*, epidemiologist Christoph Scholtissek confirms, "Because of a dense cohabitation of humans, pigs, and water fowl in China, the probability of the creation of new pandemic strains is the greatest in Southeast Asia."

Christoph Scholtissek, "Source for Influenza Pandemics," *European Journal of Epidemiology* 10 (1994): 456.

environmental factors such as air currents. . . . Experiences such as the pandemic of 1781–1782 contributed to continuing tensions and uncertainties about the transmission of disease."[13]

Flu pandemics continued to ravage Asia and Europe throughout the nineteenth century. An outbreak that lasted from 1830 to 1833 may have started in China. It then spread to the Philippines, India, Indonesia, and the Polynesian islands in the Pacific Ocean. Three separate waves of it went westward through Russia and into Europe during the winters of 1830–1831, 1831–1832, and 1832–1833. It also reached North America in 1831–1832.

In October 1889 a highly virulent strain of Asiatic flu appeared in Uzbekistan, a small country in Central Asia, and in St. Petersburg, Russia. From there, it followed railroad routes to Europe, where it quickly spread throughout the continent. It spread westward from Europe and eastward from Asia to North America by December and to South America and even Africa and Australia in the spring of 1890. Like other pandemics, it came and went in seasonal waves, one each year for four years and each one worse than the one before. By 1893 it had killed an estimated 1 million people. In Paris, France, over 5,000 people died in the six weeks between December 16, 1889, and January 31, 1890. The pandemic of 1889–1893 was the last flu pandemic of the nineteenth century. Meanwhile, scientists were making enormous strides in the knowledge and understanding of disease.

Medical Discovery Explodes

The last half of the 1800s saw significant advances in the knowledge of diseases, what caused them, and how they could be prevented. The discoveries of the 1800s built upon previous work by men such as Dutch naturalist Antoni van Leeuwenhoek, who developed the microscope and was the first to observe bacteria (although no one at the time even considered that the tiny bacteria could cause disease). In 1796 English physician Edward Jenner discovered that the viral disease smallpox could be prevented using a vaccine made from cowpox skin sores, although he did not know exactly how it worked or that smallpox was caused by a virus. Hungarian obstetrician Ignaz Semmelweis found that an often-fatal illness of new mothers called childbed fever could be drastically reduced by maintaining a clean environment and by careful hand washing.

Using these and other, earlier discoveries, French scientist Louis Pasteur developed a vaccine for rabies, another viral illness, and demonstrated that boiling

Using earlier discoveries in the field, French scientist Louis Pasteur developed a vaccine for the viral illness rabies and demonstrated that boiling water killed bacteria.

water could kill bacteria. In 1875 German scientist Robert Koch proved that the diseases anthrax, tuberculosis, and cholera were caused by bacteria. These discoveries supported the new germ theory of disease, which proposed that illnesses were caused by living organisms, and revolutionized the treatment and prevention of disease. By 1900 the causative organisms for leprosy, typhoid fever, diphtheria, tetanus, and bubonic plague had also been identified. The cause of influenza, however, remained a mystery. Before its cause was finally discovered, another flu pandemic occurred, one that has been called the worst medical disaster since the Black Death of the 1300s.

Chapter Three

The Great Pandemic of 1918

In 1918 the United States was an emerging world power despite its relatively young age of only 142 years. Immigrants from all over the world were flocking to its shores in the hopes of finding better lives than the ones they had left behind. Industry was booming, especially the war industry, as the country had recently entered World War I. Patriotism, national pride, and optimism for a bright future ran deep. It was a time of simple pleasures, of feeling safe and secure. In 1918 William Maxwell was a boy living in Lincoln, Illinois. He later recalled,

> In 1918, Lincoln was a town of 12,000 people. It was perhaps fifty years old, just time enough for the trees to mature so that the branches met over the sidewalks. Yards were large, children played in clusters in the summer evenings. On Sunday morning the church bells were pretty to hear. . . . We went fishing on Sunday, out in the country with a picnic. It was a life not very much impinged on by the outside world.[14]

That same year Cathryn Guyler was a five-year-old, living in Macon, Georgia. "It was a good world," she later recalled. "But it was an age of innocence. We really didn't know what was ahead."[15]

The Beginning

In early 1918 the local doctor in rural Haskell County, Kansas, Loring Miner, noticed that a lot of residents were coming down with the flu, but it was not the usual flu he had seen in previous years. This one was much more severe, with excruciating headaches and body aches, a high fever, and a hard, dry cough. "Miner had seen influenza often," writes flu historian John Barry. "He diagnosed the disease as influenza. But he had never seen influenza like this. This

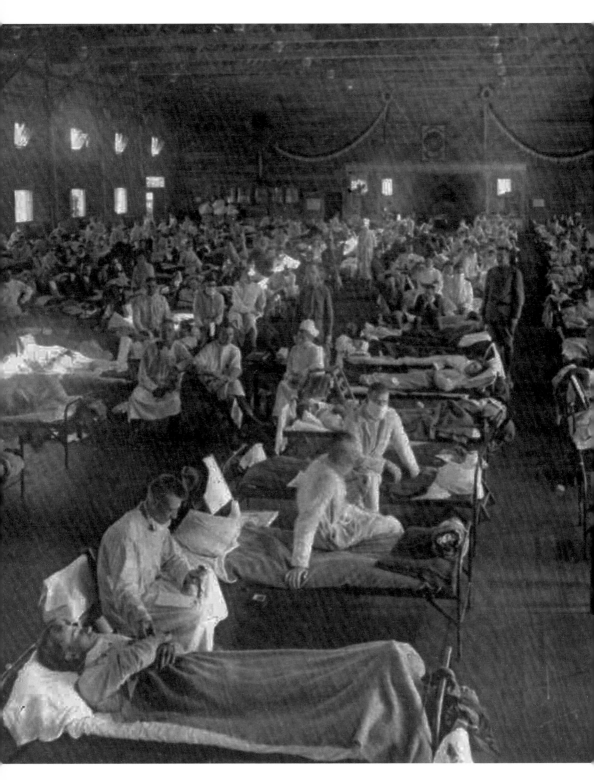

Young men from Haskell County, Kansas, convalesce in a hospital at Camp Funston near Fort Riley, Kansas. The influenza virus spread like wildfire at the military facility.

was violent, rapid in its progress through the body, and sometimes lethal. This influenza killed. Soon dozens of his patients—the strongest, the healthiest, the most robust people in the county—were being struck down as suddenly as if they had been shot."[16]

During January and February, the illness spread rapidly through the farming community's population of 1,720. Miner became overwhelmed with patients. He notified the U.S. Public Health Service in Washington, D.C. Officials there, however, were occupied with other, more pressing health issues related to the war effort, and no one was sent to Kansas to investigate. Local authorities and the local newspaper were concerned about damaging public morale during wartime, so little was reported in the papers except that someone had been ill but was recovering.

Then, in March, the outbreak seemed to end as quickly as it had begun, and residents again turned their attention to the war. Young men from Haskell County, eager to join the war effort, enlisted in the army and reported to Camp Funston, at Fort Riley military base, 300 miles (483km) to the east. Camp Funston was one of sixteen training camps constructed during World War I. Nearly 50,000 new recruits trained there from late 1917 to the end of the war in 1918.

The Flu Hits Camp Funston

The winter of 1917–1918 was one of the coldest on record. In preparation for war, men crowded by the thousands into barracks and tents, in camps with incomplete medical facilities and inadequate winter clothing and heat. That winter, an especially virulent strain of measles attacked, with soldiers dying from bacterial pneumonia infections.

Medical leaders had protested to federal authorities that the condition of the military facilities, such as Camp Funstion, created the perfect opportunity for rampant disease, but the response they got was, "The purpose of mobilization is to convert civilians into trained soldiers as quickly as possible and not to make a demonstration in preventive medicine."[17]

What Caused World War I?

World War I started in 1914, but its roots began much earlier. In the late 1800s, after the Industrial Revolution, Great Britain, Germany, and France needed new markets in which to sell their manufactured products. Germany began to fight with France and Great Britain over markets in North Africa. Meanwhile France was still angry about Germany's takeover of French territory after the Franco-Prussian War of 1870–1871. As tensions grew, a series of complicated alliances and treaties, called mutual defense alliances, were created between groups of nations. The nations in these alliances agreed to support each other in the event of an attack from another country not in the alliance.

In June 1914 Archduke Franz Ferdinand of Austria-Hungary was assassinated by a man from Serbia. Austria-Hungary declared war on Serbia. This set off a complicated chain reaction. Russia came to the aid of Serbia, so Germany (an ally of Austria-Hungary) declared war on Russia and, two days later, on France. Germany entered Belgium to attack France, prompting Great Britain to declare war on Germany. Great Britain's overseas colonies of Australia, India, Canada, New Zealand, and South Africa, offered their support. Then Japan, honoring its alliance with Britain, declared war on Germany, which prompted Austria-Hungary to declare war on Japan. Italy joined the fray in 1915. World War I had begun.

U.S. president Woodrow Wilson resisted involving the United States in the war until March 1917, when it was discovered that Germany had tried to get Mexico to join it in war on the United States. In return, Germany would help Mexico take back parts of New Mexico, Texas, and Arizona. President Wilson and Congress declared war on Germany and its allies on April 2, 1917.

Measles was not the only illness the soldiers in camp shared with each other. On the morning of March 4, the company cook at Camp Funston reported to the camp hospital with symptoms of the flu. A young corporal followed him a few minutes later. By noon that day, over one hundred ill soldiers had crowded into the camp hospital. By the end of the week, there were over five hundred. By the middle of March, eleven hundred soldiers were sick enough to be hospitalized, with thousands more ill as well. Thirty-eight of them died. Then, as in Haskell County, the illness seemed to disappear as quickly as it came. That might have been the end of it except for one thing—the war in Europe.

Influenza Leaves Camp

Once they had completed their training, soldiers from Camp Funston were sent to other army bases around the country. They could not know then that they carried the flu with them. On March 18, the first cases of influenza were reported at Camps Forrest and Greenleaf in Georgia. By the end of April, twenty-four army camps had had epidemics of influenza. Still, officials in Washington paid little attention to the epidemics taking place in the army camps. Their main concern was getting men trained and trained quickly, to be shipped overseas as soon as possible.

By this time, the sickness was out in the civilian population as well, with thirty of the largest cities in the country showing a sharp increase in deaths from influenza. Several features of this flu were very different from the usual flu. First, most of its victims were young adults at the peak of health, rather than the very young and the elderly who were the usual victims of flu. Second, many of these deaths had occurred very rapidly, within twenty-four to forty-eight hours after the first symptoms appeared. Autopsies of some of the victims showed a third very disturbing aspect of the illness—the victims' lungs had become almost completely filled with bloody fluid. Doctors could do little but treat the symptoms and watch helplessly as their patients struggled for air, their hands, feet, and faces turning a dark bluish color from lack of oxygen.

By the beginning of the summer, the terrible disease finally seemed to be going away, and the numbers of illnesses and deaths decreased. Americans breathed a sigh of relief, believing that the worst was over, and thousands of American troops shipped out to ports in Europe and Africa. The worst was yet to come, however. Sometime over that summer, the nasty flu virus of spring changed into a killer that terrorized the world.

Influenza Goes to Europe

Just as the flu was declining in the United States, it was increasing in Europe. In March and April 1918, over two hundred thousand American troops had been sent overseas, and they unknowingly carried the flu virus along with them. The first noticeable outbreaks of flu occurred in April in Brest, France, an important point of arrival for American troops. Despite high numbers of soldiers and civilians falling ill, however, few died. By the middle of April, influenza was spreading through the French army and had arrived in Paris and in Italy. It invaded the British Expeditionary Force, resulting in thousands of soldiers being hospitalized. Late in the month it hit the German military, a force already demoralized by its impending defeat in the war. Deaths still were relatively low, but the main concern for the commanders on both sides was that it severely interfered with their ability to fight.

Over the summer, influenza ran rampant throughout Europe and Asia. English troops returning from the mainland brought it back to England, Scotland, and Wales. India, as a territory of Great Britain, had become involved in the war effort, and flu arrived there late in May. Other English territories were also struck—Shanghai in May, Australia and New Zealand by September. It swept across China and North Africa. It arrived in full force in Portugal, Greece, Norway, and Denmark. It invaded Sweden and the Netherlands in August. Everywhere it went, it sickened thousands. Still, though, the death rate remained fairly low, and some doctors began to question whether it was even influenza at all. By August new cases dropped sharply, and British commanders were ready to declare the pandemic over. It was far from over.

Influenza Becomes a Killer

There is a phenomenon in the science of disease known as serial passage. This means that, as a pathogen passes from animal to animal or from person to person, it becomes weaker over time, especially if the pathogen has jumped to a new species (for example, from pigs to humans). Louis Pasteur called this "attenuation." The 1918 spring wave of influenza seems to have followed this pattern. Initially severe, over the summer its symptoms became milder, so that by August, the pandemic seemed to be coming to an end. Unknown to doctors and scientists of the time, however, was another fact about serial passage. It can also cause a virus to get stronger.

If a pathogen eventually adapts to its new host and its defenses, then it starts to strengthen as it spreads, and when fully adapted, it can become lethal. As the 1918 spring version of flu spread from person to person, it gradually adapted to the human host. The adaptation was complete by August. Having become fully adapted to its human hosts, it transformed into a version more virulent and deadly than it had been all that summer. Instead of attacking only its usual target, the trachea and its branches, this new version went much deeper—all the way into the alveoli, the tiny air sacs in the lungs where carbon dioxide is exchanged for oxygen. This newer version killed more of its victims and killed them very quickly—within twenty-four to forty-eight hours of the first symptoms. Death came from a rapidly progressing pneumonia that turned the skin a dark bluish color from lack of oxygen,

In response to the flu coming to Europe two Parisian men wear and advocate the use of masks to protect people from the spread of the Spanish flu in 1918.

caused bleeding from the nose, and filled the lungs with blood.

Isolated outbreaks of the new influenza exploded in London and Birmingham, England; in Switzerland; and in several other places in Europe. Meanwhile, throughout September, ships from Europe continued to arrive in American ports, full of soldiers returning from the war, and many of them very sick. American officials, believing that the worst of the pandemic had passed, downplayed the danger and insisted that there was no danger of a new epidemic. Just as the British army was deciding that the pandemic was over,

Influenza Gets a Nickname

Although Europeans paid more attention to the flu of 1918 than the Americans initially did, there was still little said about it. Because of their engagement in World War I, governments were very careful to restrict any information that might give the enemy a potential advantage, including information about higher than normal numbers of sick and weakened troops. Spain was an exception. Spain had remained neutral during the war, so there were no troop movements in or out of Spain. The flu came late to Spain, but by the end of June, 8 million Spaniards had died.

Because Spain was not involved in the war, the Spanish government did not censor their communications, and Spanish newspapers reported on the flu extensively, especially after the king became seriously ill with it. In the United States this gave the impression that the majority of flu cases was occurring in Spain, and the disease came to be called "Spanish flu."

bursts of deadly influenza swept once again through Brest, France, where hundreds of thousands of troops disembarked. It hit the African port city of Freetown, Sierra Leone, a major stop for coal fuel. Eventually it arrived in Boston, Massachusetts, a major port for soldiers returning home. In all three places, the ships that docked there were packed with sick and dying men.

The Flu Comes Back to America

The new outbreak of flu in Boston in late August 1918 marked the beginning of the second wave of influenza in the United States. By mid-September, two thousand naval officers and enlisted men were sick, barely able to breathe and coughing up bloody mucus. Army bases fared no better. At Camp Devens, an army camp near Boston, over 1,500 soldiers fell ill in one day. Two days later, 342 men were diagnosed with pneumonia, and 63 died. The hundreds of doctors, nurses, and aides sent to care for them also began to get sick and die. Autopsies revealed profound pneumonia, with dense, swollen, dark-bluish lungs filled with bloody fluid. The camp hospital, built to hold 1,200 patients, soon overflowed with more than 6,000. Physician Roy Grist wrote to a colleague,

These men start with what appears to be an ordinary attack of La-Grippe or influenza, and when brought to the Hosp. they very rapidly develop the most vicious type of Pneumonia that has ever been seen. Two hours after admission they have the Mahogany spots over their cheekbones, and a few hours later you can begin to see the cyanosis [blue tinge to the skin] extending from their ears and spreading all over the face. . . . It is only a matter of a few hours then until death comes. . . . It is horrible. One can stand to see one, two, or twenty men die, but to see these poor devils dropping like flies. . . . We have been averaging about one hundred deaths per day. . . . Pneumonia means in about all cases death. . . . For several days there were no coffins and the bodies piled up something fierce. . . . It beats any sight they ever had in France after a battle.[18]

At first, public officials in Boston paid little attention to the outbreak, as there were more pressing and interesting matters to attend to, such as the upcoming vote for women's suffrage (voting rights), the revolution in Russia, and the September 11 victory of the Boston Red Sox in the World Series. Also, flu was still widely considered to be little more than just a bad cold. No one had seen the flu kill like it was killing now, and many people refused to believe that this illness was really flu. Some doctors believed it was actually bubonic plague, also known as the Black Death, because of the darkening of the skin. Many people also thought of the illness as a problem for the military, but not for civilians.

Maxwell remembers, "My first intimations about the epidemic were that it was something that was happening to the troops. There didn't seem to be any reason to think that it would ever have anything to do with us. And yet, in a gradual remorseless way, it kept moving closer and closer."[19]

Not Just Soldiers

From Boston the deadly new flu spread in every direction—west to Philadelphia, Pennsylvania, and Chicago, Illinois, and south along the coast, to New Orleans, Louisiana, and beyond into Mexico. By now it had invaded the civilian population as well as the military. Those in the cities became sick first. Expanding industries, such as steel manufacturing, shipbuilding, and weapons manufacturing, had brought hundreds of thousands of people to the cities, and immigrants from all over the world were pouring into American cities in search of a better life. Most of them had little money for doctors and a limited ability to communicate with them. Overcrowded, filthy slums developed in all the major cities in the east, providing plenty of human hosts for the virus to infect.

In Philadelphia, one of the hardest-hit cities in the country, a city-wide patriotic parade took place on September 28, attended by over two hundred thousand people. Three days later, every single hospital bed in all thirty-one hospitals was filled, and hospitals began to turn sick people away. Emergency hospitals were set up in garages, vacant buildings, churches, gyms, and open parks, but there were very few doctors and nurses healthy enough to care for the sick. All public gatherings were canceled, and schools, churches, theaters, and courthouses were closed. Spitting on the ground was made illegal.

In ten days the death toll from flu went from one or two a day to hundreds every day, with hundreds of thousands of people ill. With too few undertakers, grave diggers, and caskets, bodies piled up, on porches, in yards, on streets, in back rooms, and on fire escapes. In scenes that recalled the Black Death of the fourteenth century, carts were driven through the city, house to house, collecting the wooden boxes containing the dead. Many others, with no one to take care of them, lay in the streets where they had died. Mass graves were dug using steam shovels. Whole families just disappeared. This scene was played out in cities and towns all over the United States. Children even sang this rhyme while jumping rope, "I had a little bird and its name was Enza. I opened up the window, and in-flew-Enza."

By the end of September, the flu had become a national crisis that the federal government could no longer afford to ignore. The U.S. Public Health Service (USPHS) found itself utterly unprepared to handle a crisis of this magnitude. It had appointed directors in each state to head up efforts to fight the flu, but a major problem was the severe shortage of doctors and nurses to work with them. Most of them had been sent to Europe to tend to soldiers. The nursing shortage was especially critical, because nurses were the ones actually taking care of the sick; there was little that doctors could do. Many people died from starvation or dehydration for lack of nursing care.

City and state officials across the country quickly passed laws making it mandatory for all citizens to wear cloth masks. "Obey the laws and wear the gauze, protect your jaws from septic paws,"[20] went the slogan. The masks were of little use against the flu virus, but no one could know that, because human viruses had not yet been discovered. Doctors treating the sick urged health officials to take immediate precautions to help protect civilians by imposing quarantines on the sick; closing schools, churches, and other public meeting places; and by canceling large public gatherings, but the public tended to resist such efforts. Across the nation, patriotic rallies, county fairs, parades, and other such public gatherings continued, and the flu became an indiscriminate killer of soldiers and civilians alike.

Myths and Misinformation

Contributing to the spread of the flu was a lack of useful information about influenza. By 1918 scientists knew how to develop and use vaccines to prevent bacterial illnesses. They thought the flu was caused by a bacterium that had been named *Haemophilus influenzae*. Scientists rushed to develop vaccines using that and other kinds of bacteria. They did not work, however, because the scientists

People crowd the steps of a church in Fresno, California, praying to ward off the influenza virus. Unfortunately many such public gatherings spread the virus much more quickly.

were using the wrong organism. They could not know at that time that the flu was caused by a virus. Desperate physicians all over the world, not satisfied with treating the symptoms alone, tried anything they could think of to treat or prevent the illness. Some treatments had at least some science behind them; others had no basis other than desperation, including bloodletting and the use of poisons, such as strychnine and arsenic. The cloth masks had been a dismal failure. None of the dozens of treatments the doctors tried were effective. Eventually they stopped trying.

As a result of the lack of information and the apparent failure of medical science, fear took hold, and people began to panic. Millions of people had no access to real medical care, and they were willing to try almost anything to survive the illness. "I had camphor balls [an aromatic chemical with some medicinal uses] in a little sack around my neck,"[21] says John DeLano. Harriet Ferrell remembers, "We used turpentine on sugar, we used kerosene on sugar, a few drops. You could smell this medication before you got too close to them, but it wasn't too bad because so many people had

Boys wear camphor-filled bags around their necks in an attempt to ward off the influenza bug. Many such "home" remedies were totally useless in fighting the virus.

these different type medications until we were all smelling bad."[22] Other people hung garlic around their necks. People who could not get real medicine cooked up their own home remedies on the kitchen stove. The belief was that if it smelled and tasted bad enough, it would work. Misinformation about the cause of the epidemic also circulated around the country. Many speculated that the Germans, the enemy during World War I, had put flu germs in the water. Rumors circulated that Bayer aspirin, a German product, was contaminated with flu germs. Well-known evangelist Billy Sunday preached that the flu was punishment for the sins of people. In Phoenix, Arizona, a rumor spread that dogs carried influenza. The police there killed every stray dog they saw, and people even killed their own pets.

In September 1918, 12,000 Americans died from influenza. October was even worse. In one week the death rate in Philadelphia was seven hundred times the normal rate, and by the end of the month, over 11,000 people had died there. In October alone, the flu killed over 195,000 Americans.

American Society Disintegrates

The flu was a killer in 1918, but not the same kind of killer as the war in Europe. In the war, Americans knew who the enemy was. American military strength was proving to be superior to that of the enemy, and Americans got through the war and did what they had to do with courage and confidence.

As the disease spread, Americans became too afraid to talk to each other without masks. In this photograph taken in Seattle, Washington, a pedestrian is refused a place on the trolley car because he is not wearing a mask.

The flu was a different kind of enemy. This enemy was unseen and unknown, and it was doing its killing at home. Death came quickly to friends, neighbors, and family. The worst part was that the killer came from other people—people who had been friends and neighbors. Now people were afraid to get too close to each other. Daniel Tonkel remembers, "People were actually afraid to talk to one another, it was almost like don't breathe in my face, don't look at me and breathe in my face because you may give me the germ that I don't want, and you never knew from day to day who was going to be next on the death list."[23] Long-time neighbors refused to help each other. Ill family members, including children, were sometimes abandoned because of terror of the disease. Americans wondered if anyone at all would be spared, and they were terrified.

Fear eventually turned to violence. Physician Alfred Crosby says, "An epidemic erodes social cohesiveness because the source of your danger is your fellow human beings, the source of your danger is your wife, children, parents and so on. So, if an epidemic goes on long enough, and bodies start to pile up and nobody can dig graves fast enough to put the people into them, then morality does start to break down."[24] Undertakers had to hire armed guards to prevent coffins from being stolen. In San Francisco, California, a police officer shot a man for refusing to wear a mask. In Chicago, Illinois, a man killed his own wife and children, rather than watch them die of influenza. In Alabama, a traveling salesman from Philadelphia, Pennsylvania, suspected of being a German agent, was found with his wrists and throat cut. Police called it a suicide.

Worldwide Catastrophe

While the flu was killing tens of thousands in the United States that fall, it was devastating the rest of the world as well. In Paris over forty-five hundred people died in October alone. Seventy thousand American soldiers in Europe were sick, and some units lost as much as 80 percent of their men. General John Pershing (who himself became ill with the flu, but survived) pleaded for replacements. President Woodrow Wilson thought long and hard about whether to send the troops. He knew that sending more men to Europe on crowded troop ships would certainly make matters worse. He knew that it would mean death from flu for many of them. In the end, he sent the troops. No soldiers showing signs of illness were sent, and onboard, groups of men were separated from each other behind sealed doors, but many still got sick and died, and the burials took place at sea.

The flu virus was unaffected by climate. In frozen Alaska, then a U.S. territory, native Eskimos died by the thousands, and entire villages were wiped out. Those who did not get sick died from starvation, as there were not enough healthy villagers to hunt for food. In tropical Gambia, in western Africa, influenza destroyed entire towns and hundreds of families. It killed 4 percent of the population of Cape Town, South Africa, and 10 percent in the state of Chiapas, Mexico. It killed seven out of every one hundred people in Russia and Iran. In the Pacific Ocean, ten out of every hundred died on the island of Guam, and in only sixteen days it killed 14 percent of the population of Fiji and 22 percent in Western Samoa. Worst of all was India, where over 20 million people died, and corpses clogged the rivers.

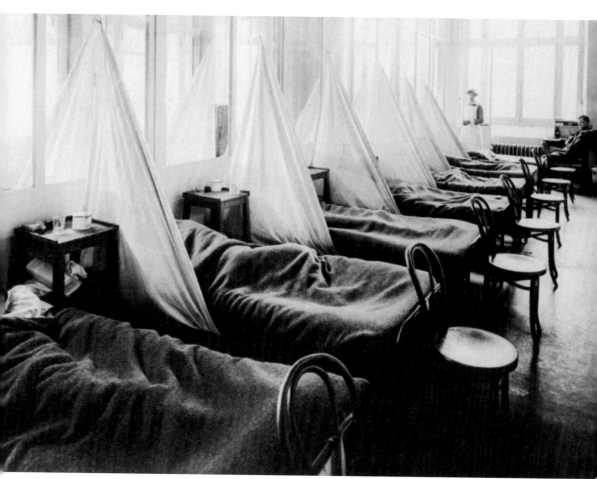

Soldiers lie in the influenza ward of a U.S. military hospital in France in 1918. Seventy thousand soldiers were affected, and some units lost 80 percent of their men to the virus.

The Flu Disappears

October 1918 marked the peak of the pandemic. In early November, what must have seemed like a miracle happened. The flu suddenly began to just go away. In cities along the eastern coast of the United States, the numbers of new cases and deaths dropped sharply. In Philadelphia deaths from flu dropped from 4,597 during the week of October 9 to almost none by November 11. One theory was that the virus simply ran out of susceptible humans to infect. Those who had survived the flu were now immune to it. Another theory is that when the supply of living hosts declined enough, the virus may have mutated again into a milder strain so as not to kill off too much of its supply. It was noted that those who became ill late in the pandemic did not get as sick and were much less likely to die than those

Modern Researchers Unlock the Mystery

E ver since the 1918 flu pandemic, researchers have been trying to determine why it was so lethal and why it killed mostly young, healthy adults. In 2005 a group of American researchers announced that they had succeeded in re-creating the 1918 virus and mapping its genetic structure. They used tissue samples from a female flu victim who had been buried in the permafrost of Alaska and from the remains of American soldiers to isolate the virus's genetic material and re-create it in the laboratory.

Since then other researchers have used the re-created strain to learn more about it. In January 2007 another American research group infected monkeys with the re-constructed strain. The monkeys quickly became very ill and exhibited signs of cy-tokine storm—a massive overreaction of the immune system. The monkeys' lungs became inflamed and filled with blood and fluids, similar to what human victims experienced in 1918. The results helped confirm the theory about why the 1918 flu killed mostly young adults: It was the response of their stronger immune systems. It is hoped that information like this can be used to help prevent deaths in the event of future flu pandemics.

Sample blocks containing lung and brain tissue from victims of the 1918 Spanish Flu pandemic were used to re-create the 1918 virus and map its genetic structure.

who had caught it earlier on. That very same month, World War I ended. In San Francisco, the citizens who remained celebrated the end of the war by dancing in the streets—still wearing their masks.

The Aftermath

The illness persisted in varying levels of severity in many parts of the world throughout 1919 and 1920. On the evening of April 3, 1919, President Wilson himself became suddenly ill while in Paris negotiating terms for the end of the war. He recovered after several days. By the time the pandemic finally ended, it had infected about 30 percent of the entire world population. Ten to 20 percent of those infected died from it. It killed more people than the Black Death of the 1300s, and more people than the AIDS epidemic of the late twentieth and early twenty-first centuries. The 1918 flu killed approximately 550,000 Americans and an estimated 50 to 100 million people worldwide at a time when the entire world population was, at just under 2 billion, less than one-third of what it is in the early twenty-first century. This influenza reached all corners of the globe, from Alaska to southern Africa to remote Pacific island villages. Thanks to a strict quarantine of arriving ships, Australia saw the flu very late and lost only about 12,000 people, and the Pacific islands of American Samoa and New Caledonia did not have a single death.

This enormous death toll was partly due to the strain's extremely high infec-tion rate; it sickened at least half of all people who were exposed to it. Also contributing to the high mortality rate was the unusual severity of the symptoms. Most of the deaths took place in one twelve-week period in the fall of 1918. Over half of the victims were between the ages of sixteen and forty. By contrast, 300,000 Americans and 15 million others died as a result of World War I. Many more people died of influenza in 1918 than died in all the wars of the twentieth century.

After the pandemic had subsided, many wondered if such a flu pandemic could ever happen again. Scientists around the world devoted themselves to making sure it could not. On December 28, 1918, the following was published in the *Journal of the American Medical Association*:

The [year] 1918 has gone: a year momentous as the termination of the most cruel war in the annals [historical record] of the human race; a year which marked the end, at least for a time, of man's destruction of man; unfortunately a year in which developed a most fatal infectious disease causing the death of hundreds of thousands of human beings. Medical science for four and one-half years devoted itself to putting men on the firing line and keeping them there. Now it must turn with its whole might to combating the greatest enemy of all—infectious disease.[25]

Chapter Four

Influenza in the Twentieth Century

Scientists and doctors of the early twentieth century knew that the horrific Spanish influenza of 1918 had been caused by a microorganism of some kind, but it was not like any microbe they had already seen under the microscope. With the development of the germ theory of disease in the previous century, followed by rapid successes in diagnosing and preventing illnesses such as cholera, tuberculosis, typhoid, and smallpox, scientists and doctors naturally began by looking for another bacterial organism to explain influenza. An early suspect was the bacterium Pfeiffer's bacillus, today called *Haemophilus influenzae*, which was found in the throats of many flu victims. Researchers working with the bacterium injected animals with it, but it did not cause flu symptoms in animals. In addition, when liquid samples containing Pfeiffer's bacillus made from the sputum of flu patients was filtered so as to strain out the bacillus, the filtered liquid could still cause the flu.

These findings essentially ruled out a bacterium as the cause of influenza. Attention then turned to viruses.

The Beginnings of Virology

Virology—the study of viruses—began long before 1918. In 1892 Dmitri Ivanovsky, a Russian botanist who was interested in diseases of the tobacco plant, was asked by the Russian Department of Agriculture to investigate a plant disease called tobacco mosaic disease, named for the spotty appearance of the disease on tobacco leaves. Ivanovsky crushed some of the infected leaves, made a liquid from them, and then forced the liquid through a very fine porcelain filter called a Chamberland filter, designed to trap bacteria. He discovered that the filtered liquid, or filtrate, still caused the disease when it was brushed on healthy tobacco leaves, although no organisms could be seen in the filtrate under a microscope. He concluded that tobacco mosaic disease was not caused by a bacterium but by some kind of toxin produced by a bacterium. Unable to identify the actual cause of tobacco mosaic disease, he eventually abandoned this work.

Six years later, in 1898, Dutch botanist Martinus Beijerinck repeated Ivanovsky's experiment and discovered that the filtered liquid did not cause the disease if it was heated. He called the filtered liquid, "contagious living fluid" and also called it "virus," from the Latin word for "toxin."

At the same time, bacteriologists Friedrich Loeffler and Paul Frosch

In 1898 Friedrich Loeffler (pictured) and Paul Frosch were able to prove that filterable viruses also caused disease in animals when they were able to cause foot and mouth disease in healthy cattle by injecting them with filtrates made from diseased cattle.

proved that these filterable viruses also caused disease in animals. They were able to cause foot-and-mouth disease in healthy cattle by injecting them with filtrates made from skin lesions on diseased cattle. By the turn of the twentieth century, several other plant and animal diseases were shown to be caused by such filterable viruses, including yellow fever in humans and "fowl plague," a form of influenza known to cause death in chickens. Still, however, the filterable viruses were thought to be liquid in nature. There was no way to know that viruses were actually particles.

Filterable Viruses and Influenza

By 1918 as the Spanish flu raced around the world, researchers raced to identify the cause of the flu once and for all, some still looking for a bacterium, others focusing on filter-passing viruses. Early in September French researchers Charles Nicolle and Charles Lebailly produced flu symptoms in both monkeys and in healthy human volunteers by injecting them with a filtrate made from the sputum of a flu patient. Over the next three months, other researchers were able to reproduce the same results, strongly suggesting that influenza was not caused by bacteria but by a filterable virus.

A Giant Leap Forward

The study of influenza took a huge leap in the 1930s. At this time, the connection between influenza in animals, such as pigs and birds, and influenza in humans was suspected, but it had not yet been confirmed. In early 1918 just before the beginning of the Spanish flu pandemic, pig farmers in the United States noted an outbreak of a respiratory illness in their pigs. Another such outbreak occurred in 1929. It was so similar to influenza in humans that it was called swine influenza.

In 1931 American doctors Richard Shope and Paul Lewis found that filtrates made from the mucus of sick pigs could cause flu in healthy pigs if it was squirted directly into the healthy pigs' snouts. In addition, they were able to transfer the illness over and over again to different pigs. This proved that a filterable virus was indeed the causative agent of swine influenza. Two years later, British researchers Wilson Smith, Christopher Andrewes, and Patrick Laidlaw conducted the same kind of experiment in humans, proving that a filterable virus was the cause of influenza in humans. The connection between flu in pigs and flu in humans was finally made when both teams were able to demonstrate that a serum (similar to a vaccine) prepared from humans who had survived the 1918 flu was effective in preventing pigs from getting swine influenza. This showed that the 1929 swine flu was closely related to the 1918 human flu and established the connection between swine and human strains. At this time, viruses were still thought to be liquid in nature.

Two very important advances were made in 1935. First, scientists began to develop a better understanding of the

A major advance in research occurred in 1935 when Dr. Wendell Stanley discovered that viruses were not liquid in nature but were molecular protein structures that required other living cells to survive.

physical components of the influenza virus. American biochemist Wendell Stanley discovered that viruses were not liquid in nature but were actually molecular structures made of protein and that they required other living cells in order to survive. Researchers in England added the finding that tobacco mosaic and other plant viruses contained the genetic molecule ribonucleic acid (RNA). Then, in 1943, scientists finally saw the object of their work, when the influenza virus was actually seen using the newly developed electron microscope. The next year, as the world waged World War II (1939–1945), a turning point came in the battle against influenza.

A Victory over Influenza

In 1925 Thomas Francis was one of the researchers working on developing a vaccine against Pfeiffer's bacillus, the organism that many scientists still believed was the cause of influenza. By the 1930s he had turned his attention to viral diseases, such as influenza and polio. In 1935 he was able to isolate the human flu virus by studying it in ferrets. Two years later he began to explore the development of a flu vaccine for humans using viral cultures instead of bacterial ones.

In 1941 Francis was appointed director of the Commission on Influenza by the U.S. Army. The United States had just entered World War II, and the army had no desire to repeat the awful experience of 1918. By 1943, Francis had a vaccine ready for use. During the last six months of 1943, over twelve thousand army personnel were vaccinated with Francis's vaccine, made from flu virus that had been killed with a chemical called formaldehyde. Formaldehyde destroys the virus's ability to cause disease but the human body still produces antibodies against it. The vaccine was so successful that the commission called for 10 million more doses to be given to military personnel, and in 1945 it was approved for use in the civilian population. Killed-virus vaccines have been in use every year since then.

The Asian Flu of 1957

After the 1918 Spanish flu, there were two more twentieth-century pandemics caused by influenza strains that started in animals, adapted to humans, and spread around the world. The first of these occurred in 1957 and came to be called the Asian flu. The Asian flu was an H2N2 strain, believed to have begun as an avian strain found in wild ducks and which, through antigenic shift, picked up five of its eight genes from an existing human strain. From there, it adapted fully to humans. As this was an entirely new strain, humans had no immunity to it, and it spread rapidly.

The pandemic started in the Guizhou Province of south-central China in early 1957. By February the flu had spread to Singapore, at the southern end of the Malaysian peninsula. It reached the Chinese port of Hong Kong by April, infecting both civilians and American naval personnel stationed on ships

The Electron Microscope

Basic microscopes use ordinary light, passed through a lens, to magnify objects. In the mid-1600s, Dutchman Antoni van Leeuwenhoek became the first person to use a microscope to see bacteria, microscopic organisms in pond water, and red blood cells moving through tiny blood vessels. Further improvements to the microscope were made by Englishman Robert Hooke and American Charles Spencer. Even the very best light microscopes in the twenty-first century, however, cannot see objects that are smaller than 275 nanometers in size. There are 25 million nanometers in 1 inch (2.5cm). The flu virus ranges in size from 50 to 120 nanometers. In order to see particles that small, a different kind of energy source was needed.

In 1931 German electrical engineers Max Knoll and Ernst Ruska invented a microscope in which the movement of electrons, the subatomic particles that circle the nucleus of an atom, is speeded up. A focused beam of these speeded up electrons is aimed at the sample to be studied. Some electrons are absorbed by the object, but others bounce off of it onto a special photographic plate that is sensitive to electrons. The scattered electrons form an image of the object being studied.

In 1937 further improvements were made by Canadian graduate students James Hillier and Albert Prebus. Their microscope could magnify objects up to seven thousand times their actual size. Hillier was the first person to create an image of the tobacco mosaic virus using his electron microscope. During his career as a physicist, Hillier continued to improve the capabilities of the electron microscope. Some of the early twenty-first century's electron microscopes are so strong that they can magnify objects up to 2 million times and give images of individual molecules and even atoms.

Ernst Ruska, right, was the inventor of the first electron microscope. Here, he checks out the first one built in Germany in 1931.

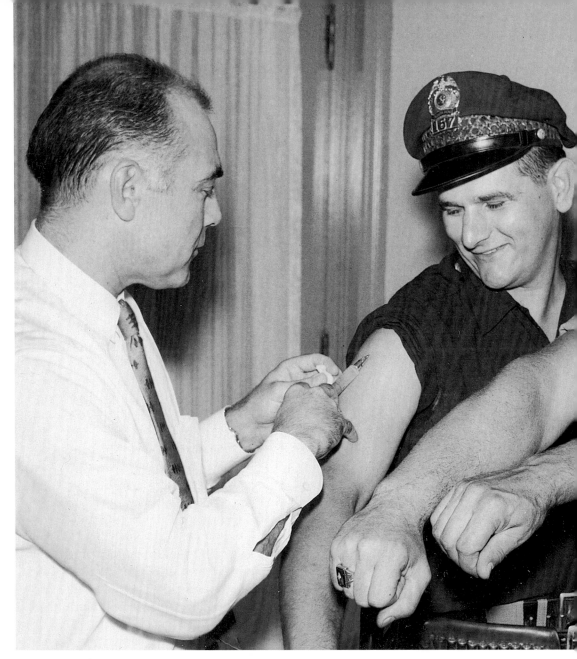

there. It broke out almost simultaneously in Taiwan, an island off the southeastern coast of China; the Philippines; Indonesia; and Japan. By May it had arrived in India and Australia. Just as in 1918, the flu traveled along military routes, and by June it had arrived in Pakistan, Saudi Arabia, and the

United States. It broke out in South America, South Africa, and New Zealand in July. In less than twenty weeks, cases were being reported around the world.

Gordon P. Fields was in the U.S. Navy in 1957. He describes his experience with the flu that year:

Members of the South Bend, Indiana, police force receive the vaccine for the Asian flu in 1957. It marked the first time an effective vaccine was available to fight the pandemic before it had run its course.

In the fall of 1957, while serving aboard USS *Barton* in the Mediterannean Sea, I experienced and survived a severe case of influenza. The ship was at Port Said, Egypt preparing to transit the Suez Canal, North to South. As the departure time of midnight approached, I began to experience the onset of flu symptoms; headache, sweating, aches and pain, blurred vision, and general discomfort. It became necessary that I be relieved from my duties so I went below to my bunk. I wrapped myself in my wool blanket because of chills and slept. Some hours later I awakened and my bedding was soaked from perspiration. I got up and passing an opened door, I recall looking out and seeing the sand bank of the canal to starboard (right side of the ship) and a man was there sitting on a camel seemingly just a few feet away from me. I may have been hallucinating, but I believe it was real and not a dream. The illness swept throughout the crew. After we had all recovered, the U.S. Navy then required mandatory inoculation [vaccination] of all personnel! For years following, all Navy personnel received mandatory annual influenza vaccination (the doctor was always set up at the head of the pay line!).[26]

The first cases in the United States appeared in a series of small outbreaks, mostly among school-age children. Larger-scale community outbreaks did not occur until the fall, when school resumed and children shared the virus with each other and their families. By October, at its peak in the United States, the flu was mostly infecting children, young adults, and pregnant women. While the elderly were not infected as often, they were more likely to die from complications, such as pneumonia, so their death rates were the highest of all groups.

Olivia Huggins was six years old and living in New Mexico at the time. She remembers,

> In 1957, I was living with my family (mother, father and six siblings) in Maxwell, New Mexico. All of us children and my mother, Elizabeth, were sick in bed with the Asian flu. My father, Manual Pacheco, survived the 1918 pandemic flu event and he didn't get sick. We were all running high fevers and did not have central heating in our home; we had a wood and coal stove. The back bedrooms, where we usually slept, were too cold, so we were all sleeping in roll–away beds near the stove. Manual kept the stove going, worked his regular job, took care of the chores on our farm, and brought us oranges to eat. I do not recall eating any meals.[27]

By 1957 medical technology had progressed enough that the new strain was identified fairly quickly by physicians at Walter Reed Army Hospital in Washington, D.C. Health officials predicted a possible pandemic. Vaccine production began within three months after the first outbreaks, and the first vaccines were available by August. This marked the first time that an effective vaccine was made available before a pandemic had run its course. By December the pandemic seemed to subside. As is typical of influenza, however, a second wave struck early in 1958. In some countries the second wave was worse than the first, especially among the elderly.

The 1957 Asian flu was a much milder pandemic than the 1918 Spanish flu, largely because so much more was known about influenza, because the new strain was identified quickly, and because an effective vaccine was made available. It was designated a category two pandemic on the Pandemic Severity Index. By the time it ended, it had infected as many as 4 million people around the world. It caused about 70,000 deaths in the United States and, according to the World Health Organization, a total of about 2 million worldwide. In contrast to the 1918 flu, most deaths occurred in people with existing health problems, such heart or lung disease.

The Hong Kong Flu of 1968

Eleven years following the Asian flu, a new flu threat emerged as a result of another shift in the genetics of the flu virus. The H2N2 virus of the 1957 pandemic had altered its HA antigen to become an H3N2 subtype, another new strain to which people had very little immunity. It had two genes from an avian strain found in ducks, and the remaining six genes were from the human strain circulating at the time.

The first cases of this flu appeared in Hong Kong in July 1968. The population in Hong Kong is very dense, averaging about five hundred people per acre, and the illness spread rapidly, reaching its peak severity in only two weeks. International efforts to learn about this new flu were complicated by the fact that China, under Communist Party chairman Mao Zedong, was now in the midst of its cultural revolution, and communication with Western countries had been severely restricted.

Very soon after its first appearance in China, cases showed up in Vietnam and Singapore. By September it had spread to the Philippines, Australia, India, and Eastern Europe. At the same time, it arrived in California, brought by American troops returning home from the Vietnam War. By December it had become widespread in the United States, with most infections occurring in December and January.

December and January also saw the peak death rates from this flu worldwide. By the time it subsided in early 1969, approximately 1 million people had died from it, including almost 34,000 in the United States. The case-fatality ratio for this pandemic was less than 1 percent, about 1 in every 200 cases, making it a category two on the Pandemic Severity Index. Most deaths were among those over sixty-five years old.

This pandemic resulted in far fewer deaths than the 1957 pandemic for several reasons. First, since the virus changed only the HA portion of its antigen makeup, from H2 to H3, and the NA portion remained the same, there may have been some resistance to the newer strain leftover in people who had the H2N2 Asian flu eleven years earlier. Although the presence of antibodies built up by the immune system in response to the 1957

Asian flu did not prevent people from getting the flu again in 1968, it did help lessen the severity of the illness the second time around. Second, medical care had improved greatly since the earlier pandemic. Third, there were more effective antibiotics available to fight secondary bacterial pneumonia. Finally, a vaccine for the virus was quickly made available.

Influenza Scares

After the 1968 Hong Kong flu pandemic, three flu scares occurred later in the century. These were considered scares rather than pandemics, because although they each presented a new strain of flu virus, they were all confined either to a particular location or to a particular group of people.

The first flu scare happened in 1976 at Fort Dix in New Jersey. Fort Dix is a basic training center for new army recruits. Training had stopped for the 1975 Christmas holiday, and when it resumed in January, a sudden outbreak of a severe respiratory illness with fever occurred, mostly among new arrivals to the fort. This happened even though the new arrivals had been given the 1975–1976 flu vaccine. An investigation began immediately, with the Fort Dix physician working closely with the New Jersey Department of Health. Lab tests revealed that two different flu strains were circulating at the fort, a known H3N2 strain and one unknown strain. By February 13 with help from the Centers for Disease Control (later renamed Centers for Disease Control

and Prevention) in Atlanta, Georgia, and the Walter Reed Army Institute of Research in Washington, D.C., the unknown strain was identified as an H1N1 strain. Genetically it was similar to the 1918 strain, and this was cause for great concern. A large-scale effort to produce vaccine for it was started, with almost 45 million Americans receiving the vaccine. As it turned out, the feared pandemic never happened.

About 230 soldiers, mostly new recruits, became ill. Four of them developed pneumonia, and only one died. The outbreak subsided by the end of February and never spread beyond the Fort Dix area. There are several possible reasons for this. First, military and civilian health officials acted quickly and cooperatively to identify the new strain and take measures to contain it. Second, the illness was confined to new arrivals at the fort, mostly young men in their late teens and early twenties. Older personnel who had been at the fort for awhile had received earlier vaccines and possibly had built up some resistance to the new strain. Third, contact between new recruits and others at the fort was very limited. Fourth, there may have been some competition for hosts between the two flu strains, with the older H3N1 strain limiting the effect of the newer strain, which had not had time to become fully adapted to humans.

After this experience, public health officials clarified what kinds of flu viruses could be considered capable of causing an imminent pandemic. Not only does the virus have to show that it

How Vaccines Are Made

Each year laboratories in different countries send several different circulating influenza virus strains to the Centers for Disease Control and Prevention (CDC) in Atlanta, Georgia. There, the viruses are tested to determine which kinds of antigens they carry. Experts at the CDC determine which of the strains represent the most potential for causing flu outbreaks in the upcoming season. This information is shared with the U.S. Food and Drug Administration (FDA) and the World Health Organization (WHO). The WHO then decides which strains should be included in that season's flu vaccine. The U.S. Department of Health and Human Services National Vaccine Program Office coordinates all the agencies involved in vaccine production and distribution worldwide.

The vaccine that is developed each year is called an inactivated trivalent vaccine. This means that it contains three different killed-flu virus strains—one influenza B strain, which, though milder than influenza A, still causes significant numbers of cases of flu each year, and two influenza A strains. How effective the vaccine is each year depends on how closely it matches the strains that actually show up that year. The match is right about 90 percent of the time.

As of 2009, there are four companies in the United States that manufacture vaccines. The viruses that are chosen for the vaccine are grown inside fertilized chicken eggs. Chicken eggs are used because they are a plentiful and inexpensive source of rapidly growing living cells for the virus to grow in. It takes about one to two eggs to produce enough of the virus to make one dose of vaccine. After several days, the viruses grown in the eggs are removed, inactivated with special chemicals, and prepared in liquid injectable form, and bottled for distribution. The whole process takes about six months and must be completed in time for the flu season, which begins in late September. Three months later, the whole process begins again for the next year.

A lab worker handles chicken eggs that are used to develop H1N1 flu vaccine at a facility in Shanghai, China.

In December 1997 a Chinese government worker sprays a poultry market to eradicate the H5N1 avian flu virus found there. Fortunately the H5N1 virus did not spread as quickly as previous bird flu viruses.

can infect people, but it must also be a novel, or brand-new, strain, and it must show that it can cause high infection and death rates in several geographic areas in one or more countries or on more than one continent. The Fort Dix flu did not meet all of those requirements.

The Russian Flu

The second flu scare occurred the very next year. In May 1977 another H1N1 flu virus caused an outbreak of influenza among children and young adults under age twenty-three in China. The Chinese cultural revolution had all but ended with the death of Mao Zedong in 1976, but his successors still maintained a policy of isolation from other nations. For this reason, the illness did not get international attention until November, when it became epidemic in Russia. By January 1978, cases had appeared around the world. In the United States, as in many other countries, it affected mostly children, young adults, and young military recruits.

The reason that the illness affected younger people is that, in 1957, the H1N1 strains that had been circulating among the population had mutated to become the H2N2 strain that caused the Asian flu and then mutated again to become the H3N2 of 1968. After 1957, there were no known H1N1 strains circulating. Therefore, those people born after 1957 had never been exposed to H1N1 strains, so they were especially susceptible to this new strain.

Even though this flu spread around the world, it affected only a very lim-

ited group of people, so it is not considered a true pandemic. One question that remains is where this H1N1 strain, genetically almost identical to those that existed before 1957, had been for twenty years. "You can anticipate certain rates of change in each gene per year, even if the hemagglutinin and neuraminidase stay the same," says Brian Murphy, chief of the respiratory virus laboratory at the National Institute of Allergy and Infectious Diseases in Bethesda, Maryland. "But this virus looked as if it was in a genetically frozen state."[28] Many flu researchers believe the 1977 strain was actually a 1950s strain that may have been released as the result of a laboratory accident in China or Russia.

The 1997 Avian Flu

In the spring of 1997, chickens at three farms in northern Hong Kong began getting sick and dying. Testing on the chickens revealed an H5N1 strain of avian influenza. Then, in May, a three-year-old boy named Lam Hoi-ka became gravely ill with an upper respiratory illness and died eleven days later from severe pneumonia. At first, tests on his tissues failed to show what caused his death, but influenza was suspected. By August the causative agent was finally identified as exactly the same avian H5N1 flu strain. It was very surprising that this avian strain had infected a human directly without first passing through and reassorting inside another mammal, such as pigs, as avian strains usually did. It turned out that the day-care center the boy attended had kept chicks and duck-lings as pets, some of which had been sick and had died.

Throughout the summer and early fall of 1997, flu almost disappeared from Hong Kong. Then, in November, another case of H5N1 flu was reported in a two-year-old boy, with two more cases soon after. Health officials were once again mystified by this virus be-cause, unlike previous flu strains, it had spread directly from birds to people. American flu expert Keiji Fukuda, at that time a member of the influenza branch of the Centers for Disease Con-trol and Prevention, was sent to Hong Kong to investigate. "Most of the time in public health and in medicine," he says, "there's a fair amount of uncer-tainty, but you rarely come across is-sues where there's a really high degree of uncertainty and what you're sitting on may be something like a 1918 [pan-demic]. You feel like, 'I don't know what is going to happen. I don't know what is going on. But what is going on is not good, and what it reminds me of is the worst not-good of the century.'"[29]

Meanwhile, as new cases continued to appear, the public began to panic. Ef-forts to develop a vaccine were ham-pered by the fact that making vaccines involves using eggs that contain un-hatched chicks, and the virus, which had already killed thousands of adult chickens before sickening humans, also killed the embryo chickens in their eggs. Without live embryo chicks for the virus to grow in, a vaccine could not be made. Fortunately, however, H5N1

was also different from other flu strains in that it did not seem to spread easily from person to person. The regular flu season was about to start in February, however, and health officials worried that the new strain might take genes from the circulating seasonal human strains and become a version that would easily spread between people.

Further investigation by health offi-cials found that the virus was now pres-ent in chickens throughout the country's live poultry markets. In response to this, international health organizations urged the Hong Kong government to order the slaughter of all chickens. Naturally local officials were reluctant to do this be-cause of the economic impact, but by the time four people had died from the flu, the decision was made. At the end of De-cember, approximately 1.5 million chick-ens and other poultry birds were slaughtered in Hong Kong. Almost im-mediately, new cases in humans stopped. A pandemic had been prevented. By that time, however, of the eighteen con-firmed cases, six had died, the last one in early January.

Lessons Learned

A 2005 report from the Center for Infec-tious Disease Research and Policy at the University of Minnesota notes that sev-eral very important lessons were learned from the three major influenza pandemics of the twentieth century. First, according to the report, "pandemics behave as un-predictably as the viruses that cause them. During the previous century, great variations were seen in mortality, severity

Reverse Genetics

Cytokines are protein chemicals that are considered the first line of defense against infections. These proteins regulate the intensity and duration of the immune response when an infection is detected in the body. One of the mysteries of the 1997 H5N1 avian flu virus was that it seemed to be able to avoid the immune system's infection-fighting cytokines. Using a technique called reverse genetics, scientists at St. Jude Children's Research Hospital in Memphis, Tennessee, came up with an explanation for how the virus was able to do this.

In traditional "forward" genetic studies, scientists start with a particular characteristic of an organism and try to find the gene responsible for it. Reverse genetics is the same process, only in reverse. —Scientists start with a particular gene and seek to determine the characteristic that the gene controls in the organism. The St. Jude scientists knew that the H5N1 virus had a mutation in a gene called the NS gene. They wanted to know what this mutation did to the behavior of the virus. They removed the gene from the virus and inserted it into another, much less virulent, strain of flu. They then infected pigs with the modified virus and found that the pigs became much sicker than pigs that had the virus without the mutated NS gene in it. Closer study of the NS gene revealed that it was able to shut down the production of cytokines in the infected pigs, thereby interfering with the pigs' immune system and making the H5N1 virus more virulent than other flu strains.

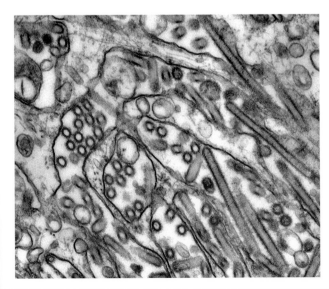

A colorized transmission electron micrograph of the H5N1 Avian flu virus is shown in gold. St Jude Children's hospital researchers were able to replace a gene in the virus that made it less virulent.

of illness, and patterns of spread."[30] On the other hand, one of the few consistencies among these pandemics was the very rapid rise in cases over a very short period of time, often just a few weeks. Another consistent characteristic of flu pandemics is that the ability of a flu strain to cause high death rates in young adults is an indicator of how severe the pandemic is likely to be over its course.

Another important lesson is that flu pandemics seem to occur in waves and that later waves tend to be more severe. This was especially apparent during the second wave of the 1918 pandemic. This feature of flu pandemics is important because it means that there may be more time for vaccine production before the most severe part of the pandemic hits. Another key lesson according to the center's report is that "most pandemics have originated in parts of Asia where dense populations of humans live in close proximity to ducks and pigs."[31] While these conditions are particularly widespread in Asia, the threat of pandemic influenza exists wherever these living conditions are present. Even the 1918 flu, which appears to have begun in the United States, started in a rural area where hog farming was a major part of the local economy. Another lesson learned is that improved public health measures have been able to delay, but not stop, the international spread of pandemics. The better a country's yearly flu vaccination program is, the more experience it will have in providing effective vaccines to safeguard its citizens and help prevent the worldwide spread of influenza.

Chapter Five

Influenza Today and Tomorrow

The twentieth century saw a revolution in the knowledge and understanding of infectious diseases in general and influenza in particular. The discovery of the existence of microorganisms, the perfection of vaccination, improvements in public health and sanitation, the development of antibiotics, and advancements in technology that allow scientists to not only see viruses but also to decipher their biological processes and behavior based on their genetic makeup all eventually led to a general feeling among the medical and scientific communities that man had conquered the lowly germ.

Having learned to control diseases like cholera, polio, plague, yellow fever, and many others, (and even eliminating one—smallpox), it was easy for the medical community to turn its attention away from infectious disease. During the 1960s, as cancer and heart disease gained more and more attention, infectious disease became less and less attractive as a field of study for new doctors. In his 1962 book, *The Natural History of Infectious Disease*, Sir MacFarlane Burnet writes, "To write about infectious disease is almost to write of something that has passed into history."[32] In 1978 the member nations of the United Nations signed the Health for All 2000 Accord, which predicted that by the turn of the twenty-first century, even the citizens of the most backward of nations would be worrying more about diseases of old age rather than infectious diseases like the flu.

But of course, infectious diseases have not disappeared. New organisms, such as human immunodeficiency virus (HIV), which causes acquired immunodeficiency syndrome (AIDS), occasionally appear. Microorganisms are extremely adaptable to the efforts of modern science to control them, and drug-resistant forms of old illnesses,

A lab technician uses a microscope to study the H5N1 virus, which appears in the monitor. The twentieth century saw a revolution in the knowledge and understanding of infectious diseases.

such as tuberculosis present an ongoing challenge. "It takes us seventeen years to develop an antibiotic," says David Morens, a medical epidemiologist at the National Institute of Allergy and Infectious Diseases (NIAID) in Bethesda, Maryland. "But a bacterium can develop resistance virtually in minutes. It's as if we're putting our best players on the field, but the bench is getting empty, while their side has an endless supply of new players."[33]

Avian Flu

The 1997 avian H5N1 flu virus is one of the "new players" described by Morens.

The 1997 flu scare in Hong Kong never turned into a pandemic, but concerns about avian flu, often called "bird" flu, still remain. Its ability to spread to humans directly from birds represents a major change in the way the flu virus has behaved in the past. While H5N1 does not currently spread easily from human to human, there is concern that the virus, with its ability to mutate so easily, may in the future adapt to become a form that can spread between humans and against which the body has no defense.

Another feature of avian H5N1 flu that makes it so worrisome is that it attacks the body differently from ordinary seasonal flu. Seasonal flu, the kind that appears every year, normally attacks the upper parts of the respiratory tract—the nose and throat. This causes the symptoms of sniffles and a dry cough. Avian H5N1 flu, however, invades the body much farther, going deep into the lungs, all the way in to where the critical exchange takes place between oxygen and carbon dioxide. There, the virus replicates extremely rapidly, destroying the delicate lung cells and breaking down the lung tissue. As the lungs deteriorate, the infected person may begin to cough up blood and may bleed from the nose and mouth.

H5N1 also does not stop at the lungs. It can attack the intestinal tract, kidneys, liver, heart, and even sometimes the eyes and brain. In its desperation to control the infection, the immune system can go into overdrive and result in the potentially deadly cytokine storm. For this reason, H5N1 tends to be most deadly to younger people, who have more robust immune systems. All these features of H5N1 avian flu bear a striking resemblance to those of the 1918 Spanish influenza pandemic.

Avian H5N1 flu is endemic, which means it is always present in many different species of birds, especially poultry, such as chickens. It is especially present in Southeast Asian countries, such as China and Indonesia, where thousands of poultry birds, both sick and well, are brought in from outlying farms to large open poultry markets in the cities. In 2001 another strain of H5N1 appeared in chickens in Hong Kong. As in 1997, over 1 million market chickens were slaughtered. In addition, a new regulation was put in place that requires all unsold live poultry to be removed from the markets and killed and the stalls cleaned one day each month to help prevent the spread of viruses among the birds. Yet another strain appeared in 2002, but it never again jumped from chickens to people. The H5N1 flu virus continues to circulate in the poultry population of this area of China, constantly drifting and shifting into new and different versions of the virus. Some flu experts insist that the poultry markets of Hong Kong should be permanently closed. Since they are a valuable economic part of the Hong Kong culture, however, there is little chance that this will ever happen.

With the emergence of H5N1 avian flu in humans in 1997, this strain of flu became the focus of attention for many scientists and health officials around the world. As the virus spread among bird populations around the world, it gradually became more deadly to them and began to spread more easily among them. It even infected some mammals, such as tigers and leopards. "The virus has evolved in alarming ways in domestic poultry, migratory birds, and humans in just the last four years," said Margaret Chan, former director of the Hong Kong health department and now director-general of WHO, in 2007. "Global spread is inevitable."[34]

Other flu experts, although agreeing that another flu pandemic will eventually happen, disagreed that H5N1 was a serious threat. They point out that since 1997, tens of millions of birds have been infected with the virus and it has not caused a pandemic yet. "If it was going to happen, it would have happened already," says Peter Palese, a physician at Mount Sinai School of Medicine in New York. "I feel the virus is awful for chickens. But this is not a virus that has been shown to really cause disease in humans except in unusual circumstances when the dosage [of virus] has been extraordinarily high."[35] Still, Chan remains concerned about H5N1. "If you put a burglar in front of a locked door with a sack of keys and give him enough time, he will get in," she says. "Influenza viruses have a sack of keys and a bag full of tricks. They are constantly mutating, constantly delivering surprises."[36]

H5N1 is not the only avian flu strain that concerns public health officials. Since 1999, an H9N2 subtype has infected people in Hong Kong and China and has become endemic in birds across Asia, Europe, and Africa. Both H5N1 and H9N2 have shown that avian strains of flu do not necessarily have to reassort in another animal in order to sicken humans. Virus expert Robert G. Webster says, "Common

In 1997 and 2001 millions of chickens in China were slaughtered and disposed of in an effort to curb the spread of the avian virus.

sense tells me that both the H5N1's genome, and the H9N2, have something very special. They have special characteristics that allow them to spread to humans."[37] Webster believes that the "something very special" has to do with something inside the virus rather than with the HA and NA antigens on the surface. Yet another subtype, a group of H7 strains, is circulating in birds in North America and Europe. Although H7s are fairly harmless to people, they are still being monitored for changes that could make them more likely to become a threat.

Pandemic Preparedness

After the frightening 1997 avian flu scare, health officials in many countries became so convinced that another significant flu pandemic would eventually strike that they began work on formally written plans to prepare for it. Influenza preparedness plans try to include all the possible ways a flu pandemic could begin, where it could originate, how it might spread, and how modern medical technology would fight it. As more is learned about the virus, these plans are modified to keep them up-to-date.

In the United States, the Department of Health and Human Services (HHS) has developed a Pandemic Influenza Plan that

is a blueprint for pandemic influenza preparation and response. It provides guidance to national, state, and local policy makers and health departments. The HHS plan includes an

overview of the threat of pandemic influenza, a description of the relationship of this document to other Federal plans and an outline of key roles and responsibilities during a pandemic. In addition, it specifies needs and opportunities to build robust preparedness for and response to pandemic influenza.[38]

The HHS plan has three components that outline plans and provide guidance for each level of government, from federal to state to local health departments and agencies, so that everyone involved in dealing with a possible flu pandemic is familiar with their roles and responsibilities.

Pandemic Alert Level

The influenza preparedness plan drawn up by the World Health Organization (WHO) in 2005 and updated in 2009 includes flu centers in eighty-three countries, including the United States, working together to quickly analyze and identify any new strains of flu that show up. The plan outlines pandemic preparedness based on the Pandemic Alert Level. The Pandemic Alert Level is a tool for describing how serious a pandemic, or potential pandemic, is at any given time. It divides a pandemic into six numbered phases. The higher the number, the more concern there is and the more action governments take to control the outbreak. Phases one through three address preparedness for a potential pandemic when there has been an outbreak mostly in animals but few if any cases in humans. The yearly seasonal spread of ordinary flu is usually phase three. Phases four through six address the response to an epidemic that has begun, with reported cases of widespread transmission between humans. Phase five is declared when there have been outbreaks in several countries. It means that a true pandemic is imminent. Phase six is declared for a global outbreak—a full-scale pandemic. An additional post-peak phase addresses the potential of the virus (or a newly mutated form of it) to reappear in more waves after the initial pandemic has started to subside. The post-pandemic phase considers the pandemic to be over and the virus to behave more like a regular seasonal flu. It is still watched closely, however, for signs of another wave.

The H1N1 Pandemic of 2009

Chan and others were correct when they predicted that another influenza pandemic would happen. In March and April 2009, an illness resembling influenza appeared in Vera Cruz, Mexico. It caused a local epidemic that lasted for several months before it came to the attention of the Mexican government. In Mexico City schools and universities were closed, and people began wearing masks when out in public.

By the end of April, the causative organism had been identified as a novel strain of H1N1 influenza, and work on a vaccine began immediately. The new strain was found to contain genes from five different other flu virus strains—an American swine flu, an avian flu, a human flu strain, and two other swine strains that were not normally seen outside Europe and Asia. Further study of the virus showed that it contained proteins that were similar to those found in strains that usually cause mild symptoms in people. Many experts concluded from this that the new strain would have little impact on humans. The new virus mostly infected younger people between ages five and twenty-four. Pregnant women and people with other health conditions had the highest risk for developing flu-related complications.

On April 27, the WHO raised the Pandemic Alert Level from phase three to phase four and called it "a public health emergency of international concern."[39] Only two days later it was raised to phase five. "Based on assessment of all available information, and following several expert consultations, I have decided to raise the current level of influenza pandemic alert from phase 4 to phase 5," said Chan. "All countries should immediately activate their pandemic preparedness plans. Countries should remain on high alert for unusual outbreaks of influenza-like illness and severe pneumonia."[40] By then the WHO had confirmed 91 cases in the United States and 236 cases worldwide. The WHO also began distributing 5 million treatment courses of the antiviral medication Tamiflu (a treatment course is about ten capsules), which had been donated by the manufacturer, Roche Laboratories.

Margaret Chan, director-general of the World Health Organization, declared a swine flu pandemic and raised the Pandemic Alert Level to six in response to an outbreak of swine flu in seventy-four countries in 2009.

By May, cases had also been reported in Canada, Spain, and Scotland, with suspected but unconfirmed cases in several other countries. The European Union health commissioner advised people in European countries to restrict unnecessary travel to the United States and Mexico. Russia, South Korea, and China began screening all new arrivals from the two countries for signs of illness.

On June 11 when almost thirty thousand cases had been confirmed in seventy-four countries, the WHO announced that the pandemic could not be contained and raised the Pandemic Alert Level to phase six, although it did not recommend closing borders. "The world is now at the beginning of the 2009 influenza pandemic," said Chan. "The scientific criteria for a pandemic has been met." She also pointed out another concern about this pandemic: "We need to continue to check this virus and monitor it. We should never forget . . .

Epidemiology

Epidemiology is the study of factors that affect the health of a population. It looks at how diseases spread among populations, what parts of the population are most at risk for an illness and most affected by it, how the nature of the illness changes over time, and how it can best be controlled. Epidemiologists are health professionals who study these factors and use what they discover to recommend public health policy and treatment methods. They work very closely with government and other health experts whenever and wherever an outbreak of a disease occurs. Well-known epidemiologists include Briton John Snow, considered to be the founder of modern epidemiology for his exhaustive work in controlling a nineteenth-century cholera outbreak in London, England, and Hungarian Ignaz Semmelweis, who instituted disinfection procedures to lower infant mortality in Vienna, Austria.

Epidemiologists are actively involved in many aspects of influenza research, especially pandemic influenza. For example, a project called the Resistance of Influenza Viruses in Environmental Reservoirs and Systems is under way in tropical countries with the goal of understanding the role of environment—water, air, soil, housing, etc.—in the survival of the flu virus and in the occurrence of outbreaks. Other scientists are studying how the flu virus circulates in other animals, especially birds and pigs. Still others are looking at the effect of flu in specific populations, such as children or the elderly.

Epidemiology is the study of how diseases spread among populations, how they change over time, and how best to control or eliminate viruses.

we still have H5N1 in phase 3 pandemic alert status, and this is the first time we have two viruses coexisting. . . . It is an extremely unusual situation."[41] In July when the number of cases reached ninety thousand, the WHO stopped keeping track of individual cases except when they appeared in previously unaffected countries.

The Vaccination Effort

The 1997 avian flu scare had prompted many countries around the world to develop and perfect pandemic preparedness plans, so many were already well prepared when the novel H1N1 virus appeared in Mexico in 2009. One of the most critical parts of the plans was to control the spread of the virus and minimize deaths through the development and distribution of an effective vaccine.

The regular yearly vaccine for the seasonal 2008–2009 flu had already been prepared when the H1N1 flu gained attention. Because H1N1 was not circulating when the seasonal vaccine was made, it was not included in the vaccine. An entirely new vaccine had to be prepared for H1N1. The work proceeded very quickly in an effort to get the vaccine ready before the beginning of the fall flu season, but it was still put through the same rigorous testing for safety and effectiveness that the regular flu vaccine undergoes every year. As the summer passed, people all over the world were anxious for the vaccine to be ready.

Four companies worked on producing the vaccine. It was prepared in two forms—an injectable form, or flu shot, and a spray form called FluMist that could be sprayed into the nose. The spray form was available first. It was made from a live but weakened form of the virus and was considered to be more effective for children and younger adults. The injectable form was made from a killed virus and was recommended for older adults.

The vaccines were approved for use by the U.S. Food and Drug Administration on September 15, 2009, and the first doses were made available in early October. Supplies of vaccine were very limited at first, so the Centers for Disease Control and Prevention (CDC) made recommendations about who should receive the vaccine first. The list of first recipients included pregnant women, people who live with or care for children under age six, health-care and emergency services workers, people between the ages of six and twenty-four, and older people with chronic health disorders. The CDC recommended that after these groups received the vaccine, it should be made available to all others who wanted it. It stressed that the H1N1 vaccine was not a substitute for the seasonal vaccine, and that people should get both vaccines. By late fall, there was enough vaccine for everyone who wanted it, both in the United States and around the world. The H1N1 strain is now included in the seasonal vaccine for the 2010–2011 flu season.

The Pandemic Subsides

By the time the H1N1 vaccine was available in October 2009, almost all reported cases of flu were H1N1 flu. Over

Emerging Infectious Diseases

Influenza is not the only infectious disease that concerns world health officials. Infectious diseases are a continuing danger to everyone. Some diseases, such as smallpox, have been controlled with the help of modern technology. New diseases, however, such as severe acute respiratory syndrome (SARS) and West Nile virus, are constantly appearing. These new diseases are referred to as emerging diseases. SARS first appeared in humans in 2003. That year it sickened eight thousand people and caused 774 deaths. It is caused by a new version of a virus called a coronavirus. Early symptoms of SARS are similar to influenza, but about 20 percent of victims also develop diarrhea. Most also develop pneumonia. There is no specific treatment except for supportive care in an intensive care unit.

West Nile virus was first identified in Uganda in 1937. It appeared in the United States in 1999. The next year, it began to appear in birds and mosquitoes. It is transmitted to humans by ticks and mosquitoes. According to the Centers for Disease Control and Prevention (CDC), it caused 3,404 cases in 2007 and ninety-eight deaths. Symptoms are very similar to influenza, with the addition of a possible skin rash and are normally mild unless the virus enters the brain, where it can cause severe encephalitis or meningitis. Currently there is no vaccine or medication for West Nile virus.

Other emerging (and older, reemerging) diseases of interest include dengue, Lyme disease, plague, prion diseases such as mad cow disease, and botulism. Organizations such as the CDC, the World Health Organization, and the National Institute of Allergy and Infectious Diseases support ongoing research into these and other emerging infectious diseases.

340,000 confirmed cases of H1N1 had been reported to the WHO, with over forty-one hundred deaths. In November the pandemic began to slow down as numbers of new confirmed cases began to decline. In January 2010 Chan said that the pandemic seemed to be subsiding in the Northern Hemisphere but could still cause infections into April. By then, over fourteen thousand people had died. Chan also said that it was too soon to know what would happen as Southern Hemisphere countries entered their winter.

As of May 2010, the WHO had reported that over 201 countries and territories had reported cases of H1N1 flu and that there had been over eighteen thousand deaths. H1N1 flu is still active in many parts of the world, and the most active areas are parts of western and central Africa, the Caribbean, and Southeast Asia. The WHO continues to monitor the circulation of all types of influenza, including H1N1.

Influenza Research

In the twenty-first century research on influenza focuses on many aspects of the disease. For example, molecular virology studies the composition of the flu virus at the molecular level. Viral genomics looks at how the genetic structure of the virus causes its behavior. Research in these and other areas help scientists and doctors understand the flu virus more completely so that future pandemics can be prevented, and if they do occur, they can be better controlled with safer and more effective vaccines provided in a more timely manner to those most in need or at higher risk.

New Ways to Diagnose Influenza

Currently the diagnosis of influenza is based mainly on the set of symptoms that it causes. If a diagnostic test is needed to confirm the particular strain

A scientist uses a portable testing machine that recognizes influenza viruses at the molecular level. The briefcase-size machine can be used all over the world and can indentify a virus in one hour.

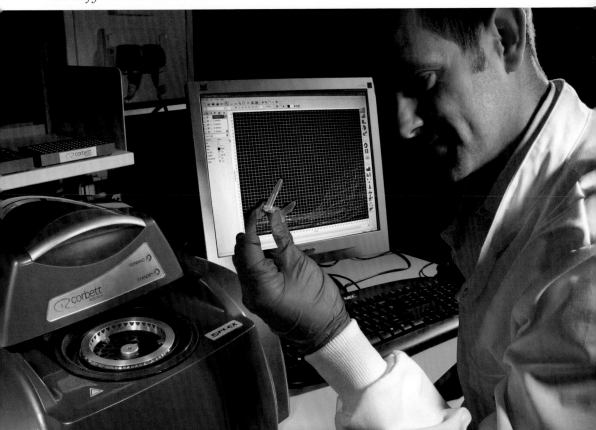

of flu, a swab of the nose or throat is taken and sent off to a laboratory, possibly miles away from the doctor's office. It can take weeks for the result, and by then the illness has run its course in the patient and may have spread to many hundreds or thousands of others.

In order to be better prepared for a pandemic, health officials need a quicker way to know exactly what kind of flu strain they are dealing with so that vaccine production can begin quickly. Several researchers are working toward this goal. Scientists at the medical technology company InDevR have developed a device they call a "flu chip" that can analyze gene activity in the virus and provide information about which strain it is in about an hour. The device is about the size of a deck of cards. It analyzes the virus using a technique called DNA microarray technology. In this process, short segments of specially marked DNA genetic material are placed on a glass slide. When the ribonucleic acid (RNA) from a particular flu virus is added to the slide, it will stick to the strands of deoxyribonucleic acid (DNA) in a very characteristic way for that particular strain and begin to glow a bright yellow. Using the pattern of yellow strands, scientists can tell if a virus is influenza A, B, or C. It can also tell the subtype of an influenza A virus— whether it is H1N1, H5N1, etc.

The flu chip can also be used to detect viruses for respiratory diseases besides influenza. It is small enough that it can easily be sent to laboratories in any part of the world where a flu outbreak is emerging. So far, the flu chip has proven to be highly accurate in detecting specific subtypes of influenza.

Research on the Influenza Virus

One of the most active areas of flu research is aimed at learning more about the virus itself—its structure and how it behaves. In 2008 scientists at the NIAID discovered a new viral protein in the influenza A virus that can apparently destroy immune system cells, making the virus much more deadly. The new protein, called PBI-F2, is coded by a gene that, until the discovery of the protein, was "camouflaged" behind a much larger gene. PBI-F2 also attacks the host cell's mitochondria, the parts of a cell that produce most of its energy, causing the host cell to die sooner.

Scientists at two research centers are working together to see if there may be a better way to attack flu viruses with vaccines. Current vaccines target the HA and NA antigens on the surface of the virus. The problem is that these antigens are changing constantly through antigenic drift and reassortment. Another surface protein, however, called the M2 protein, stays the same from year to year. The M2 protein is essential for the virus to "uncoat" itself inside the host cell and inject its genetic material into the cell. Because the M2 protein does not change from year to year like the HA and NA proteins do, a vaccine that targets the M2 protein could be effective against all kinds of flu strains.

The M2 protein is also the target for the antiviral drugs amantadine and rimantadine, but these drugs are not used much anymore because most flu viruses, through mutation of their genetics, have developed resistance to them. A 2004 study found that flu viruses may also be developing resistance to NA inhibitors, such as Tamiflu. The study showed an increase in the resistance to the drugs from earlier studies, suggesting that influenza may be developing resistance to both classes of antiviral drugs. If this finding is confirmed, it will mean that different antiviral drugs may be needed in the future. Other researchers, meanwhile, are studying the M2 protein to find out how genetic mutations allow the virus to avoid the effects of the drugs, so that more effective drugs can be made.

Research on Vaccines

Influenza vaccines have been available since the 1940s. The traditional method for developing a vaccine is to grow cultures of the virus in chicken eggs, purify the cultured virus, inactivate them chemically, and prepare them for distribution. This process takes at least six months and

Swine flu H1N1 vaccine is manufactured at the Sanofi-Pasteur production plant in France. The company's vaccines are used worldwide.

The Influenza Sequencing Genome Project

A genome is a complete listing of all the genes on all the chromosomes in a particular organism that determine how the organism looks, how it behaves, and how its cells work. For example, the human genome consists of twenty to twenty-five thousand genes on forty-six chromosomes. The Influenza Sequencing Genome Project is a project designed to provide data about the genomes of all known influenza viruses to international researchers working on increasing knowledge about the virus—how it mutates, causes disease, and spreads. The goals of the project are to learn more about the virus so that future epidemics and pandemics can be minimized and to improve development of influenza medications and vaccines.

A group of scientists who saw the need for a full listing of influenza genomes as well as a way to make the information accessible to scientists around the world began the project in November 2004. By the following year, they had published a report containing descriptions of over one hundred influenza genomes. In 2006 an Italian research group joined the project and contributed their collection of avian flu genomes, including several H5N1 strains. As of April 2010, the project had 5,048 human and avian strains of influenza sequenced and available to world researchers.

requires millions of eggs. New methods of diagnosing specific flu strains are contributing toward the goal of shortening that process.

Since the 1990s, researchers have been working on a method to grow viral cultures using tissue cells rather than chicken eggs. Kidney cells from mammals, such as dogs, are the preferred type of cells for this method. The virus to be cultured is injected into the cells, and as the virus multiplies inside the cells, the cells themselves also grow, divide, and multiply. The advantage to this method is that it takes less time to get finished vaccine because, unlike eggs, the cells can multiply along with the virus inside

them. Another advantage is that production could be more easily sped up in the event of an emerging pandemic. Disadvantages are that the cell-based method costs a great deal more than the egg-based method, and it may produce somewhat less vaccine. Cell-based flu vaccine production is still experimental, but all major vaccine producing companies are working on perfecting it.

Using Reverse Genetics to Build a Vaccine

Another method that may help speed up vaccine production is reverse genetics. Scientists used this technique to discover what made the H5N1 avian flu so

Cells are observed in cultures of live swine influenza virus. The virus will be used in reverse genetic techniques to produce a specialized flu vaccine.

deadly to humans. Researchers are now seeing if the same technique can be used to create a custom-made vaccine.

With egg-based viral cultures, three different viral strains are injected into an egg, where they multiply and naturally go through reassortment—in other words, they trade genes with each other. When the cultures are ready, the scientists have to sift through all the reassorted viruses to find the ones that have the particular HA and NA antigens that they want for that year's vaccine. With reverse genetics, scientists can build their own vaccine by putting together only the genes that code for the right antigens. The scientists extract two genes from the virus that is targeted for that year—one gene for the HA antigen and one for the NA antigen. They add six more genes from another flu strain that has shown that it can grow well inside an egg. The combined genes are put into animal cells, where the custom-made virus grows and multiplies. The viruses are then injected into eggs for the actual vaccine production.

One great advantage to this technique, besides the time saved by not having to search for the right antigens, is that if the targeted flu strain is too toxic to the chicken egg, as was the H5N1 virus, the genes that cause it to be so toxic can be removed, making the virus safer for the egg so that more virus can be grown in it.

Influenza is indeed a wily adversary. It seems to have the ability to evade even the most up-to-date science and technology by constantly changing its own genetic structure. It takes tens of thousands of lives each year and sickens countless others. But our ability to fight it also constantly changes to keep up, and ongoing research and public education provide the tools with which to control this tiny and very ancient foe.

Notes

Introduction: Not Just a Bad Cold

1. Madeline Drexler, *Secret Agents: The Menace of Emerging Infections*. Washington, DC: Joseph Henry Press, 2002, p. 161.
2. Quoted in Drexler, *Secret Agents*, p. 165.

Chapter One: What Is Influenza?

3. Quoted in Drexler, *Secret Agents*, p. 9.
4. Robert G. Webster and Elizabeth Jane Walker, "Influenza," *American Scientist* 91, no. 2 (March–April 2003): 122.
5. Quoted in Drexler, *Secret Agents*, p. 169.
6. Jan Gurley, "Ask the Doc: How Exactly Can Flu Kill a Healthy Person?" *San Francisco Chronicle*, June 5, 2009, www.sfgate.com/cgi-bin/blogs/gurley/detail?blogid=114&entry_id=41223.

Chapter Two: Influenza in the Past

7. Quoted in R.S. Gottfried, "Population, Plague, and the Sweating Sickness: Demographic Movements in Late Fifteenth Century England," *Journal of British Studies* 17, no. 1 (Autumn 1977): 19.

8. John Caius, "A Boke, or Counseill, Against the Disease Commonly Called the Sweate, or Sweatyng Sicknesse," in *The Epidemics of the Middle Ages*, 3rd ed., by J.F.C. Hecker and trans. B.G. Babington. London: Trübner, 1859. Also available at http://books.google.com/books?id=4gMAAAAAYAAJ&jtp=323#v=onepage&q&f=false.
9. Quoted in Francisco Guerra, "The Earliest American Epidemic—the Influenza of 1493," *Social Science History* 12, no. 3 (Autumn 1988): 309.
10. Quoted in Guerra, "The Earliest American Epidemic—the Influenza of 1493," p. 311.
11. Quoted in John M. Barry, *The Great Influenza: The Epic Story of the Deadliest Plague in History*. New York: Penguin, 2004, p. 113.
12. Quoted in Barry, *The Great Influenza*, p. 113.
13. J.N. Hays, *Epidemics and Pandemics: Their Impacts on Human History*. Santa Barbara, CA: ABC-CLIO, 2005, p. 172–173.

Chapter Three: The Great Pandemic of 1918

14. Quoted in *American Experience: Influenza 1918*, DVD, directed by Robert Kenner, Arlington, VA: PBS, 1998. Also available at http://pbs.org/wgbh/americanexperience/influenza.

15. Quoted in *American Experience*.
16. Barry, *The Great Influenza*, p. 93.
17. Quoted in Barry, *The Great Influenza*, p. 148.
18. Quoted in Barry, *The Great Influenza*, p. 188.
19. Quoted in *American Experience*.
20. Quoted in James F. Armstrong, "Philadelphia, Nurses, and the Spanish Influenza Pandemic of 1918," Navy Department Library, November 7, 2005.
21. Quoted in *American Experience*.
22. Quoted in *American Experience*.
23. Quoted in *American Experience*.
24. Quoted in *American Experience*.
25. Quoted in Molly Billings, "The Influenza Pandemic of 1918," Human Virology at Stanford (Web site), June 1997. http://virus.stanford.edu/uda.

Chapter Four: Influenza in the Twentieth Century

26. Quoted in Centers for Disease Control and Prevention, ed., "Pandemic Influenza Storybook." www.cdc.gov/about/panflu/stories/1957_fields.html.
27. Quoted in Centers for Disease Control and Prevention, ed., "Pandemic Influenza Storybook."
28. Quoted in Robin Marantz Henig, "The Flu Pandemic," *New York Times Magazine*, November 29, 1992. www.nytimes.com/1992/11/29/magazine/the-flu-pandemic.html.
29. Quoted in Alan Sipress, *The Fatal Strain: On the Trail of Avian Flu and the Coming Pandemic*. New York: Penguin, 2009, p. 68.
30. Center for Infectious Disease Research and Policy, "Pandemic Influenza." www.cidrap.umn.edu/cidrap/content/influenza/panflu/biofacts/panflu.html?pagewanted=4l.
31. Center for Infectious Disease Research and Policy, "Pandemic Influenza."

Chapter Five: Influenza Today and Tomorrow

32. Quoted in Drexler, *Secret Agents*, p. 6
33. Drexler, *Secret Agents*, p. 16.
34. Quoted in Sipress, *The Fatal Strain*, p. 62.
35. Quoted in Sipress, *The Fatal Strain*, p. 61.
36. Quoted in Sipress, *The Fatal Strain*, p. 62.
37. Quoted in Drexler, *Secret Agents*, p. 193.
38. U.S. Department of Health and Human Services, "HHS Pandemic Influenza Plan." www.hhs.gov/pandemicflu/plan.
39. Quoted in CNNhealth.com, "WHO Raises Pandemic Flu Alert Level; More Swine Flu Cases Feared," CNNhealth.com, April 27, 2009. www.cnn.com/2009/HEALTH/04/27/swine.flu/index.html?iref=all search.
40. Quoted in Continuity Central, "WHO Raises Pandemic Alert Level to Phase 5," April 29, 2009. www.continuity central.com/news04537.html.
41. Quoted in Emma Hitt, "WHO Increases Pandemic Alert Level to Phase 6," Medscape Medical News, June 11, 2009. www.medscape.com/viewarticle/702144.

Glossary

antibodies: Chemicals that attack and destroy foreign proteins such as viruses.

antigen: Proteins on the surface of a microorganism that stimulate the immune system to produce antibodies against the antigen.

antigenic drift: The process in which a flu virus changes its genetic makeup and creates a new strain of itself which may not be recognized by the human immune system.

antigenic shift: The process in which a flu virus picks up pieces of genetic material from other animals and adds them to its own, creating an entirely new subtype.

attenuation: The process of weakening a virus to make it less likely to cause illness.

avian: Having to do with birds.

bacteriophage: A virus that uses a bacterium as its host cell.

capsid: The protein covering that protects the viral genetic material in its center.

case-fatality ratio: The number of deaths from a disease compared to the total number of cases reported.

contagion: Anything that spreads disease organisms, such as droplets sneezed or coughed out by an ill person, or the disease organism itself.

culture: A method of growing microorganisms so they can be studied or used to make a diagnosis of illness or a vaccine for the illness.

cytokines: Immune system cells that are produced in response to an infection and stimulate the release of other types of immune cells.

cytokine storm: A serious and potentially deadly malfunction of the immune system in which it produces too much cytokine, leading to an overproduction of immune cells and significant damage to the body.

deoxyribonucleic acid (DNA): A very long, double-stranded molecule that is the main component of genes and carries the genetic code for all characteristics of living organisms.

encephalitis: An inflammation of the brain and surrounding membranes.

endemic: Always present in a certain animal or plant population.

epidemic: An outbreak of a disease in which a higher number of people or animals is affected than what is considered normal for that disease.

epidemiology: The study of the factors that affect the health or illness of a particular population.

filterable virus: The early term used to describe fluids that had been filtered so as to trap bacteria, but could still cause disease.

genes: The basic unit of genetics. A segment of DNA that codes for a particular characteristic of an individual organism.

genome: The total set of genes in a particular organism. There are twenty thousand to twenty-five thousand genes in the human genome.

germ theory: The theory that many diseases are caused by microscopic organisms.

host: The cell or organism that is invaded by a virus.

infectious: An illness that can be spread among people or animals.

lipid envelope: The protective layer that surrounds the flu virus while it is not inside a host cell.

M2 protein: A surface protein on the flu virus that allows the virus to release its genetic material into the host cell.

meningitis: An inflammation of the meninges, the membranes that surround the brain and spinal cord.

mutation: A change in the structure of a gene that changes the characteristic coded for by that gene.

Orthomyxoviridae: The family of viruses to which influenza belongs.

pandemic: A large-scale, worldwide outbreak of a disease.

pathology: The study of the causes, effects, and treatment of diseases.

pneumonia: A serious complication of some illnesses in which all or part of the lungs fill with fluid so that they cannot carry on their normal function.

reassortment: The process in which a virus picks up pieces of genetic material from other organisms and incorporates them as its own, thereby significantly changing its own characteristics.

replicate: To reproduce, or make more copies of something.

reverse genetics: A method of learning about the function of a gene by removing it from or adding it to a cell to see how it changes the behavior of a cell.

Reye's syndrome: A very serious medical condition, common in children, thought to be caused by taking aspirin during a viral illness.

ribonucleic acid (RNA): Long molecule of genetic material which is similar to DNA except that it is single stranded and contains the sugar ribose instead of deoxyribose.

serial passage: The passage of a virus through multiple hosts.

strain: A particular version of a virus within a subtype.

subtype: A type of influenza A named according to its HA and NA antigens.

vaccination: The administration of a vaccine in order to prevent a person or animal from contracting the disease for which the vaccine is made.

vaccine: A killed or weakened form of a microorganism which, when injected, stimulates the immune system to make antibodies against the microorganism and makes the person immune to the disease.

virology: The study of viruses.

virulent: Highly infectious and causing severe symptoms.

virus: A submicroscopic particle capable of causing disease.

For More Information

Books

Faith Hickman Brynie, *101 Questions About Your Immune System*. Minneapolis, MN: Twenty-First Century Books, 2000. This is a clearly written book that addresses the most common questions about the immune system.

Connie Goldsmith, *Influenza: The Next Pandemic?* Minneapolis, MN: Twenty-First Century Books, 2007. This is a comprehensive look at influenza that provides the history of the disease as well as information about current strains, treatment, and preparedness. It includes stories about the experiences of five teens and a list of supplies to have in case of a pandemic.

Denise Grady, *Deadly Invaders: Virus Outbreaks Around the World, from Marburg Fever to Avian Flu*. Boston: Kingfisher, 2006. The author describes her experience as a reporter covering an outbreak of Marburg fever in Angola, then addresses other infectious illnesses, such as SARS, avian flu, and West Nile virus.

Paul Kupperberg, *The Influenza Pandemic of 1918–1919*. New York: Chelsea House, 2008. This is a captivating account of the deadliest influenza pandemic in history.

Angela Royston, *Colds, the Flu, and Other Infections*. Mankato, MN: Smart Apple Media, 2008. This book describes the causes, symptoms, and treatment of colds and flu and how to prevent them.

DVD

American Experience: Influenza 1918, DVD, directed by Robert Kenner, Arlington, VA: PBS, 1998. Also available at http://pbs.org/wgbh/american experience/influenza.

Websites

Centers for Disease Control and Prevention (www.cdc.gov). This site provides lots of information about seasonal influenza, avian flu, swine flu, H1N1, and pandemic flu.

FLU.GOV (www.flu.gov). Provided by the U.S. Department of Health and Human Services, this site offers information about seasonal as well as pandemic flu to the public, health and emergency preparedness agencies, government and business leaders, schools, and local communities.

The Great Pandemic: The United States in 1918–1919 (http://1918.pandemic flu.gov). Provided by the U.S. Department of Health and Human Services, this is a very interesting and comprehensive site about the 1918 flu pandemic. It offers information about life in 1918 and about the impact of the pandemic in each state.

KidsHealth (http://kidshealth.org). This site offers information for parents, kids, and teens about a wide variety of health issues, including influenza and other infectious diseases.

Index

Picture Credits

About the Author

Lizabeth Hardman received her bachelor of science in nursing from the University of Florida and her bachelor of science in secondary education from Southwest Missouri State University. She has been a practicing surgical nurse for thirty years. Hardman writes stories and articles for adults and children. She lives in Springfield, Missouri, with her two daughters, Rebecca and Wendy; two dogs; two cats; and two birds. When not working or writing, she enjoys reading, hiking, and watching baseball games. *Influenza Pandemics* is her eighth book for Lucent Books.